Primary Sources

Primary Sources

Titles in the Indigenous Peoples of North America series Include:

Primary Sources

James D. Torr, Editor

Lucent Books, Inc.
10911 Technology Place, San Diego, California 92127

Picture Credits

Cover photo: © Hulton/Archive by Getty Images
© Bettmann/CORBIS, 28, 76, 88
© CORBIS, 74, 83
Denver Public Library Western History Department, 23
DigitalStock, 78
Dover Publications, Inc., 45
© Hulton/Archive by Getty Images, 12, 32, 37, 41, 81
Library of Congress, 17, 20, 31, 49, 64, 69, 71
North Wind Picture Archives, 44
© Baldwin H. Ward & Kathryn C. Ward/CORBIS, 55

Library of Congress Cataloging-in-Publication Data

Indigenous peoples of North America: primary sources / [edited]
by James D. Torr
    p. cm. — (indigenous peoples of North America)
Includes bibliographical references and index.
Summary: Examines Native American beliefs, culture, and relationships
with white men since colonial times through documents written by men
and women of various tribes.
    ISBN 1-59018-010-0 (alk. paper)
    1. Indians of North America—History—Sources—Juvenile literature.
[1. Indians of North America—History—Sources.] I. Torr, James D.,
1974– II. Series.
    E77 .I49 2002
    970' .00497—dc21

                                                        2001004224

Copyright 2002 by Lucent Books
10911 Technology Place, San Diego, California 92127

Printed in the U.S.A.

Contents

Foreword

North America's native peoples are often relegated to history—viewed primarily as remnants of another era—or cast in the stereotypical images long found in popular entertainment and even literature. Efforts to characterize Native Americans typically result in idealized portrayals of spiritualists communing with nature or bigoted descriptions of savages incapable of living in civilized society. Lost in these unfortunate images is the rich variety of customs, beliefs, and values that comprised—and still comprise—many of North America's native populations.

The *Indigenous Peoples of North America* series strives to present a complex, realistic picture of the many and varied Native American cultures. Each book in the series offers historical perspectives as well as a view of contemporary life of individual tribes and tribes that share a common region. The series examines traditional family life, spirituality, interaction with other native and non-native peoples, warfare, and the ways the environment shaped the lives and cultures of North America's indigenous populations. Each book ends with a discussion of life today for the Native Americans of a given region or tribe.

In any discussion of the Native American experience, there are bound to be sim-

ilarities. All tribes share a past filled with unceasing white expansion and resistance that led to more than four hundred years of conflict. One U.S. administration after another pursued this goal and fought Indians who attempted to defend their homelands and ways of life. Although no war was ever formally declared, the U.S. policy of conquest precluded any chance of white and Native American peoples living together peacefully. Between 1780 and 1890, Americans killed hundreds of thousands of Indians and wiped out whole tribes.

The Indians lost the fight for their land and ways of life, though not for lack of bravery, skill, or a sense of purpose. They simply could not contend with the overwhelming numbers of whites arriving from Europe or the superior weapons they brought with them. Lack of unity also contributed to the defeat of the Native Americans. For most, tribal identity was more important than racial identity. This loyalty left the Indians at a distinct disadvantage. Whites had a strong racial identity and they fought alongside each other even when there was disagreement, because they shared a racial destiny.

Although all Native Americans share this tragic history they have many distinct differences. For example, some tribes and individuals sought to cooperate almost immediately with the U.S. government while others steadfastly resisted the white presence. Life before the arrival of white settlers also varied. The nomads of the Plains developed altogether different lifestyles and customs from the fishermen of the Northwest coast.

Contemporary life is no different in this regard. Many Native Americans—forced onto reservations by the American government—struggle with poverty, poor health, and inferior schooling. But others have regained a sense of pride in themselves and their heritage, enabling them to search out new routes to self-sufficiency and prosperity.

The *Indigenous Peoples of North America* series attempts to capture the differences as well as similarities that make up the experiences of North America's native populations—both past and present. Fully documented primary and secondary source quotations enliven the text. Sidebars highlight events, personalities, and traditions. Bibliographies provide readers with ideas for further research. In all, each book in this dynamic series provides students with a wealth of information as well as launching points for further research.

— superior weaponery
— tribal identity more important
   than racial

Timeline

1872–1874
White hunters greatly reduce the buffalo population of the Great Plains.

1519–1521
A Spanish expedition under the leadership of Hernán Cortés conquers the Aztec Empire and claims Mexico for Spain.

1864
Several hundred peaceful Cheyenne men, women, and children are massacred by U.S. troops at Sand Creek, Colorado.

1830
Congress passes the Indian Removal Act, which establishes an Indian Territory in present-day Oklahoma and forces Indian tribes east of the Mississippi to relocate to the West.

1638
In perhaps the first establishment of an Indian reservation, English colonists confine the Quinnipiac to twelve hundred acres of land in Connecticut.

1450	1500	1550	1600	1650	1700

1607
Powhatan Indians save the first permanent English colony at Jamestown, Virginia, by providing food and teaching the colonists to cultivate corn.

1810–1813
Shawnee chief Tecumseh attempts to forge an alliance of Indian tribes to resist white expansion into the Great Lakes region.

1492–1500
Christopher Columbus becomes the first European to make contact with Native Americans.

1860–1890
The building of a network of transcontinental railroads encourages white settlers to move into most of the remaining Indian lands. The greatest number of conflicts between Native Americans and the U.S. government, often called the North American Indian Wars, occur in these three decades.

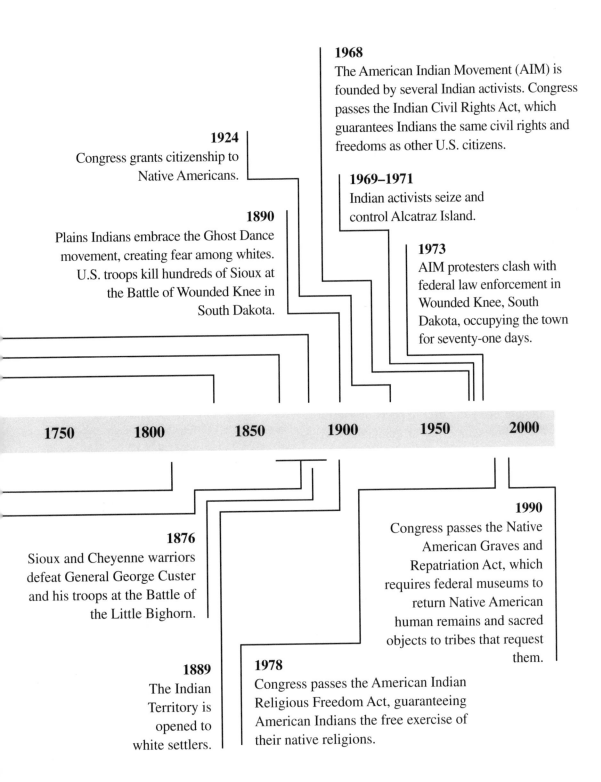

1968
The American Indian Movement (AIM) is founded by several Indian activists. Congress passes the Indian Civil Rights Act, which guarantees Indians the same civil rights and freedoms as other U.S. citizens.

1924
Congress grants citizenship to Native Americans.

1969–1971
Indian activists seize and control Alcatraz Island.

1890
Plains Indians embrace the Ghost Dance movement, creating fear among whites. U.S. troops kill hundreds of Sioux at the Battle of Wounded Knee in South Dakota.

1973
AIM protesters clash with federal law enforcement in Wounded Knee, South Dakota, occupying the town for seventy-one days.

| 1750 | 1800 | 1850 | 1900 | 1950 | 2000 |

1876
Sioux and Cheyenne warriors defeat General George Custer and his troops at the Battle of the Little Bighorn.

1990
Congress passes the Native American Graves and Repatriation Act, which requires federal museums to return Native American human remains and sacred objects to tribes that request them.

1889
The Indian Territory is opened to white settlers.

1978
Congress passes the American Indian Religious Freedom Act, guaranteeing American Indians the free exercise of their native religions.

Chapter 1

Native American Beliefs and Culture

Native American religious traditions are very different from those of Christianity, Judaism, and other major religions. One reason for this is that Native American cultures do not draw a clear line between religion and everyday life. Aspects of life that other cultures may view as mundane—such as the weather, or sickness and health—have spiritual meaning for Native Americans. Because Native Americans view their beliefs as a way of life rather than a theology, non-Indians often speak of Native American "religious traditions" rather than "religions."

Native American religious traditions place a great deal of importance on rituals. These rituals may be performed as a group (for example, the sun dance performed every summer by the Plains Indians) or individually (for example, the various rites a hunter performs after a kill). In many cases rituals are tied to a specific place, such as a hill, river, or clearing in a forest. This is one reason that many American Indian tribes fought to remain on their traditional homelands, and why it was so devastating when they were forced to move.

While Native Americans consider these observances more important than detailed religious doctrines, Native American cultures, like

A Blackfoot participates in the sun dance, a traditional ritual that signifies the transformation of a man to a warrior.

other cultures, have a variety of myths that explain why the world is the way it is. Among Native Americans, these stories were traditionally handed down from generation to generation by word of mouth; white anthropologists were often the first to write them down. In addition to their venerable oral tradition, Native Americans may also gain new spiritual insights through visions that come to specific individuals. Many tribes have a vision quest ritual in which individuals go into a dream or trance in the hope of experiencing a vision.

There are many common themes in Native American religious traditions. However, it is important to keep in mind that there are hundreds of different Native American tribes in North America, each with its own set of beliefs and traditions. They are living religions, practiced by hundreds of thousands of people, and they continue to evolve and change. The documents in this chapter provide just a few examples of the many different Native American beliefs and traditions.

A Yuki Creation Myth

The Yuki are a tribe of California Indians who were almost completely annihilated by white settlers during the California gold rush of 1849–1850. Today about fifty surviving Yuki live on the Round Valley Hill Reservation in the area once occupied by their ancestors in northern California. About thirty more live off the reservation.

In their creation myth, the Yuki envision the world being sung into creation by the creator, Taiko-mol.

In the very beginning, foam was floating around on the surface of fog-covered waters. Then a voice came from the foam, and it was followed by Taiko-mol, who had eagle feathers on his head. Taiko-mol, the creator, stood on the moving Foam and he sang as he created. In the darkness he made a rope, and he laid it out north to south. Then he walked along the rope, coiling it as he went and leaving behind it the created earth.

He did this four times and each time the water came and overwhelmed the new land. As he walked, he wondered if there wasn't a better way. Then he made four stone posts and secured them in the ground in each of the four directions. He attached lines to these posts and stretched them out across the world, as a plan. Finally he spoke the Word, and the earth was born. Next he secured the world from the waters at the edge by lining it with whale hide. He shook the earth to see if it was secure—this was the first earthquake. And earthquakes ever since that time are Taiko-mol testing his work again.

David Leeming and Jake Page, *The Mythology of Native North America.* Norman: University of Oklahoma Press, 1998.

The Trickster in Tlinget Lore

Trickster is one of the most important mythological figures in Native American cultures. He takes many different forms in different

Native American traditions, often appearing as a coyote, a wolverine, a spider, or a rabbit. In this creation myth of the Tlinget people of the Northwest Pacific Coast, he appears as a raven who brings light into the world. This Tlinget myth is similar to the ancient Greek myth of Prometheus, who stole fire from the gods and brought it to earth.

There was no light in this world, but it was told him [Raven] that far up . . . was a large house in which some one kept light just for himself.

Raven thought over all kinds of plans for getting this light into the world and finally he hit on a good one. The rich man living there had a daughter, and he thought, "I will make myself very small and drop into the water in the form of a small piece of dirt." The girl swallowed this dirt and became pregnant. When her time was completed, they made a hole for her, as was customary, in which she was to bring forth, and lined it with rich furs of all sorts. But the child did not wish to be born on these fine things. Then its grandfather felt sad and said, "What do you think it would be best to put into that hole? Shall we put in moss?" So they put moss inside and the baby was born on it. Its eyes were very bright and moved around rapidly.

Round bundles of varying shapes and sizes hung about on the walls of the house. When the child became a little larger it crawled around back of the people weeping continually, and as it cried it pointed to the bundles. This lasted many days. Then its grandfather said, "Give my grandchild what he is crying for. Give him that one hanging on the end. That is the bag of stars." So the child played with this, rolling it about on the floor back of the people, until suddenly he let it go through the smoke hole. It went straight up into the sky and the stars scattered out of it, arranging themselves as you now see them. That was what he went there for.

Some time after this he began crying again, and he cried so much that it was thought he would die. Then his grandfather said, "Untie the next one and give it to him." He played and played with it around behind his mother. After a while he let that go up through the smoke hole also, and there was the big moon.

Now just one more thing remained, the box that held the daylight, and he cried for that. His eyes turned around and showed different colors, and the people began thinking that he must be something other than an ordinary baby. But it always happens that a grandfather loves his grandchild just as he does his own daughter, so the grandfather said, "Untie the last thing and give it to him." His grandfather felt very sad when he gave this to him. When the child had this in his hands, he uttered the raven cry, "Ga," and flew out with it through the smoke hole. Then the person from whom he had stolen it said, "That old manuring raven has gotten all of my things."

John Reed Swanton, *Tlinget Myths and Texts.* Bulletin 39. Washington, DC: Bureau of American Ethnology, 1909.

 ## A Cautionary Cheyenne Myth

The Cheyenne story reprinted here is a good example of a cautionary myth of the end of the world. In it a giant, snow-white beaver sits at

the base of a post at the North Pole. The post is what holds up the world. Whenever Beaver gets angry at humanity, he gnaws at the post. When the pole is totally eaten through, the world will end. The myth warns that the pole is already halfway gnawed through.

There is a great pole somewhere, a mighty trunk similar to the sacred sun dance pole, only much, much bigger. This pole is what holds up the world. The Great White Grandfather Beaver of the North is gnawing at that pole. He has been gnawing at the bottom of it for ages and ages. More than half of the pole has already been gnawed through. When the Great White Beaver of the North gets angry, he gnaws faster and more furiously. Once he has gnawed all the way through, the pole will topple, and the earth will crash into a bottomless nothing. That will be the end of the people, of everything. The end of all ends. So we are careful not to make the Beaver angry. That's why the Cheyenne never eat his flesh, or even touch a beaver skin. We want the world to last a little longer.

Richard Erdoes and Alfonzo Ortiz, eds., *American Indian Myths and Legends.* New York: Pantheon, 1984.

 ## An Apache Vision of the End of the World

This myth of the end of the world comes from the Chiricahua Apache people of the Southwest. Living in a dry climate, the Chiricahua predict that the waters of the earth will dry up and people will kill each other off over dwindling water supplies. The story ends with a line about Native Americans

and white people trading places in a new world that will come after this one.

The old people used to tell us that when the end of the earth is coming all the water will begin to dry up. For a long time there will be no rain.

There will be only a few places, about three places, where there will be springs. At those three places the water will be dammed up and all the people will come in to those places and start fighting over the water.

That's what old Nani used to tell us. Those old Indians found out somehow, I don't know how. And the way it looks, I believe it is the truth.

Many old Chiricahua used to tell the same story. They say that in this way most of the people will kill each other off. Maybe there will be a few good people left.

When the new world comes after that the white people will be Indians and the Indians will be white people.

Morris E. Opler, "Myths and Tales of the Chiricahua Apache Indians," *Memoirs of the American Folkore Society,* vol. 37, 1942.

 ## A Cherokee Myth of Good and Evil

Different cultures explain the existence of good and evil in different ways. In the Christian religion, for example, there is the story of Adam and Eve and their exile from the Garden of Eden. Among the Cherokee, evil is symbolized by the Uk'ten', a giant, horned, snakelike monster who inhabits deep lakes, swamps, and rocky mountain passes. In this story, a boy discovers Thunder and the

Uk'ten' engaged in battle, and the boy helps Thunder win. As a result, Thunder is a friend of the Cherokee. This is symbolized whenever there is a thunderstorm: Lightning—which symbolizes the Uk'ten'—always follows Thunder.

I don't know very much: now I'm very old. I have forgotten a lot, although I've heard a lot of talking that was done long ago about the beginning of things.

For instance, everything used to talk long ago. And also when they were bringing up their boys long ago there were supernaturally wise men, and they also used bows and arrows all the time.

Here is one thing that I have heard about that I have stored away: Thunder and water work together when it rains; and since Thunder is always with us, he and we work together.

Long ago there was a boy out walking, hunting with his bow and arrows. He was on the top of a rough, rugged hill. From where he was, he heard, somewhere down below where it was even more rugged, a thundering, and he was very anxious to find out what caused it.

In looking for it, he arrived down in the valley, and in the ruggedest place [there] Thunder and an Uk'ten' (he was from the sea) had hold of each other in a fierce fight. Thunder was underneath: the Uk'ten' was so long and so strong—that's why he was able to overcome Thunder.

The boy looked at them fighting. (It was thundering very low.) When the boy was seen, when Thunder looked at him,

Thunder said, "Nephew, help me! When he looks at you, he will kill you!"

And then the Uk'ten' said, "Nephew, help me! When he thunders, he will kill you!"

They both kept saying these things.

Because Thunder was being bested, the boy felt sorry for him. He decided to shoot at the Uk'ten'. When he shot the Uk'ten', he [the Uk'ten'] was weakened. Then a second time he pulled his bow. The Uk'ten' was weakened even more and Thunder was becoming stronger. He made his thunders louder, and on the fourth thunder, the fiercest ever heard, he killed the Uk'ten'.

Thunder won, and the boy had helped him [to win]. That is the reason why to this day it thunders [all] around us: we [Thunder and man] are still together. A human being helped him.

Thunder is not fierce, but is very friendly and kind of heart because he knows that it was a little boy who saved him. (But he can become fierce if he does not like something.) He is really very friendly because he knows that it was a human being who saved him.

If the Uk'ten' had overcome Thunder, if Thunder had been shot, I suppose that the Uk'ten' would be lurking about everywhere. I wonder what it would have been like: Thunder would have killed us whenever it thundered, and an Uk'ten' can kill you just by smelling you.

Jack F. Kilpatrick and Anna G. Kilpatrick, *Friends of Thunder: Folktales of the Omaha Cherokee.* Norman: University of Oklahoma Press, 1994.

The Sacredness of the Hunt

Native American cultures recognize that in order to survive they must kill other living things. Many Native American cultures believe that animals sacrifice themselves so that humans can survive. Because of this, they viewed hunting as a sacred act: The proper rituals must be followed, or the animals might withhold their sacrifice. In this passage, James Paytiamo of the Acoma Pueblo describes a deer hunt. He details some of the elaborate rituals that must be observed before and after a deer is killed.

When we reach our camp, the first evening after dark, each one goes off in some direction by himself, to pray to strange gods. We pray towards any direction in which we think there may be some god listening to hear our prayers. We pray to the mountain lion, eagles, hawks, wolves, and other wild beasts. Then we bury our prayer-sticks and pick up a piece of log and sprinkle it with cornmeal, and say to it: "You be the deer

Florida Indians disguise themselves with deerskins to get closer to their prey.

17

which I expect to bring into camp," and then we carry this piece of wood in and place it on the campfire, and blow our breath on a pinch of cornmeal in our hands and throw it on the flames. Doing so we receive power, and hunt well.

Then each is seated on his rolled-up blanket around the campfire. The next thing we do is to choose our officers. First we choose the field chief, Tsa-ta-ow-ho-tcha. He has to see that all the hunters get their deer. If one of the hunters is unlucky enough not to get a deer, he has to divide up with him. Next we elect our governor, Dta-po-po. He is to see that the camp is in order, and keep peace in the camp. . . .

After these officers are elected, the field chief gives orders to put down as an altar, between us and the fire, the flint and other stone animals which every hunter carries with him to the hunt, and which are handed down in each family. After all of these little animals are placed on the level ground, they sprinkle white cornmeal over them, and around them, forming a circle of cornmeal. Then a song is sung which means: "We welcome this altar into our camp. Come and take a place with us." Then they sing to the mountain lion to take its place, then the wolf, then the man himself, then the owls, then the hawks. Song after song continues through the night until dawn. In the morning, each one picks up his little hunting animal, and ties it in the handkerchief around his neck, and takes his cornmeal from the little bag at his side. Praying to the strange gods, and breathing his breath on the cornmeal, he sprinkles it out to the east to the sun. . . .

When an Indian has hit a deer, he runs to the fallen animal. First he takes a small branch of a tree and brushes him off, as he has a religious belief that the deer is made of sheets of clouds, and he has to brush off the clouds to get at him. Then he reaches down in his pocket for some yellow pollen he has collected from flowers, takes it between his thumb and forefinger, drops a little on the deer's mouth, then carries it to his own breath, and makes a sign with the pollen towards the hunter's camp, which is supposed to lead the spirit of the deer to the camp.

Then he pulls the deer around by the forelegs, until he lies with his head towards the camp. The next thing is to take the little flint animals in the shapes of lions, wolves and bears, as many as he carries, and place them on the deer to feed and get back the power they gave him. They always come first. While these animals are on the deer, the hunter rolls a cigarette of cornhusks, and while he smokes he talks to the dead creature just as if he were telling a human where to go. When he finishes he gathers his flint animals, carefully places them in his bag, and talks to them while he puts them in the bag, telling them that he hopes for the good luck of another deer. Then he ties the bag with these animals round his neck under his shirt. . . .

After skinning the deer and placing the meat on these juniper twigs, the hunter starts to cut the animal into parts like a beef. He is always sure that he takes the entrails out first. He digs in the ground a shallow hole, and washes his hands. If there is no water nearby, he wipes his hands on a cloth. He reaches down with his hands into the blood and dips it up four times, and places it in the shallow hole on the earth. This is to feed the mother earth. Then he takes out the spleen, and places it nearby on a twig of a tree to feed the crow. Then he cuts him up. . . .

After each hunter gets one deer, they agree on a day to start home. Coming home they will all join in on their new songs, singing as loudly as they can, and if they camp again before reaching home, the burdens of the burros and horses are placed in line, so as to be easy to repack in line in the morning.

When they are within a mile from home, each of the hunters loads his gun with one shot, and they are fired off, one by one, so that each family by counting the shots, can tell which group of hunters is returning. As they come home each hunter makes a round circle from fir trees, to fit his head, puts evergreens on his horse's bridle, and around the deer heads. Even the burros' heads are decorated with fir twigs.

When they arrive home there will be relatives there to take charge of the meat, and see to the unsaddling and feeding of the animals. All the hunter does is to tell his wonderful story.

James Paytiamo, *Flaming Arrow's People*. New York: Dodd, Mead, 1932.

 ## Coming of Age Among the Paiute

Sarah Winnemucca Hopkins was a Northern Paiute who toured the United States in the 1880s, making speeches arguing for Indian rights. She published a book, Life Among the Paiutes, *in 1883. In the passage excerpted here, she discusses Paiute child-rearing practices and traditional puberty customs and courtship festivals, which emphasize proper behavior and the close ties among family members. She draws a contrast between traditional Indian life as she has known it and what she sees as the selfish and rude behavior of white people.*

Our children are very carefully taught to be good. Their parents tell them stories, traditions of old times, even of the first mother of the human race; and love stories, stories of giants, and fables; and when they ask if these last stories are true, they answer, "Oh, it is only coyote," which means that they are make-believe stories. Coyote is the name of a mean, crafty little animal, half wolf, half dog, and stands for everything low. It is the greatest term of reproach one Indian has for another. Indians do not swear,—they have no words for swearing till they learn them of white men. The worst they call each is bad or coyote; but they are very sincere with one another, and if they think each other in the wrong they say so. . . .

The grandmothers have the special care of the daughters just before and after they come to womanhood. The girls are not allowed to get married until they have come to womanhood; and that period is recognized as a very sacred thing, and is the subject of a festival, and has peculiar customs. The young woman is set apart under the care of two of her friends, somewhat older, and a little wigwam, called a teepee, just big enough for the three,

An Indian woman and child scan their surroundings. Native Americans value a strong family unit.

is made for them, to which they retire. She goes through certain labors which are thought to be strengthening, and these last twenty-five days. Every day, three times a day, she must gather, and pile up as high as she can, five stacks of wood. This makes fifteen stacks a day. At the end of every five days the attendants take her to a river to bathe. She fasts from all flesh-meat during these twenty-five days, and continues to do this for five days in every month all her life. At the end of the twenty-five days she returns to the family

lodge, and gives all her clothing to her attendants in payment for their care. Sometimes the wardrobe is quite extensive.

It is thus publicly known that there is another marriageable woman, and any young man interested in her, or wishing to form an alliance, comes forward. But the courting is very different from the courting of the white people. He never speaks to her, or visits the family, but endeavors to attract her attention by showing his horsemanship, etc. As he knows that she sleeps next to her grandmother in the lodge, he enters in full dress after the family has retired for the night, and seats himself at her feet. If she is not awake, her grandmother wakes her. He does not speak to either young woman or grandmother, but when the young woman wishes him to go away, she rises and goes and lies down by the side of her mother. He then leaves as silently as he came in. This goes on sometimes for a year or longer, if the young woman has not made up her mind. She is never forced by her parents to marry against her wishes. When she knows her own mind, she makes a confidant of her grandmother, and then the young man is summoned by the father of the girl, who asks him in her presence, if he really loves his daughter, and reminds him, if he says he does, of all the duties of a husband. . . .

At the wedding feast, all the food is prepared in baskets. The young woman sits by the young man, and hands him the basket of food prepared for him with her own hands. He does not take it with his right hand; but seizes her wrist, and takes it with the left hand. This constitutes the marriage ceremony, and the father pronounces them man and wife. . . . When they are married they give away all the clothing they have ever worn, and dress themselves anew. . . .

Our boys are introduced to manhood by their hunting of deer and mountain-sheep. Before they are fifteen or sixteen, they hunt only small game, like rabbits, hares, fowls, etc. They never eat what they kill themselves, but only what their father or elder brothers kill. When a boy becomes strong enough to use larger bows made of sinew, and arrows that are ornamented with eagle-feathers, for the first time, he kills game that is large, a deer or an antelope, or a mountain-sheep. Then he brings home the hide, and his father cuts it into a long coil which is wound into a loop, and the boy takes his quiver and throws it on his back as if he was going on a hunt, and takes his bow and arrows in his hand. Then his father throws the loop over him, and he jumps through it. This he does five times. Now for the first time he eats the flesh of the animal he has killed, and from that time he eats whatever he kills but he has always been faithful to his parents' command not to eat what he has killed before. He can now do whatever he likes, for now he is a man, and no longer considered a boy. If there is a war he can go to it; but the Paiutes, and other tribes west of the Rocky Mountains, are not fond of going to war. . . .

My people teach their children never to make fun of any one, no matter how they look. If you see your brother or sister doing something wrong, look away, or go away from them. If you make fun of bad persons, you make yourself beneath them. Be kind to all, both poor and rich, and feed all that come

to your wigwam, and your name can be spoken of by every one far and near. In this way you will make many friends for yourself. Be kind both to bad and good, for you don't know your own heart. This is the way my people teach their children. It was handed down from father to son for many generations. I never in my life saw our children rude as I have seen white children and grown people in the streets.

Sarah Winnemucca Hopkins, *Life Among the Paiutes*. New York: Putnam, 1883.

 ## The Sun Dance

The sun dance, performed annually every summer, is one of the most important rites among Plains Indian peoples. It is performed for the regeneration of the earth, the continuance of the people, the healing of the sick, and other blessings. In the account below, Shoshone chief Dick Washakie describes his tribe's version of the dance. The Sioux, Arapaho, Cheyenne, and Plains Cree tribes have similar observances.

The sun dance, which perhaps some of the white people have witnessed or heard tell of, has always been considered one of the most heathenish [irreligious] and most barbarous and unchristian ceremonies ever participated in by the savages, as we red men have been termed by many of our white brothers, who, I must say, have failed to make themselves thoroughly acquainted with the sacred and religious beliefs of our so-called sun dance. We indians call it the "fasting dance." Our sun dance in reality, according to our indian beliefs, is in religious beliefs, the same as that of our white brothers. The indians pray to God, our Father above, or the Great Spirit, as some of our white brothers have termed it. Some white people have even accused the indian of worshipping the center sun dance pole, which is a great mistake. When the indian prays, he looks upward into the blue sky and says, "Tomah-upah tomah-vond, Our Father, who is above." He does not pray to the sun, or to the center sun dance pole as some white people would have it.

The reason the indian seems to worship the sun to some people is because the indian believes that the sun is a gift from God, our Father above, to enlighten the world and as the sun appears over the horizon they offer up a prayer in acceptance of our Father's gift. Then the medicine man, or the chief of the sun dance who acts similar to that of the priest or clergyman in a white man's church, offers up prayer beginning thus "Tomah-upah, tomah-vond undidda-haidt soonda-hie, Our Father who is above, have mercy upon your children."

The sun dance hall (an out-of-doors structure) is constructed in a large circular corral perhaps some hundred feet in diameter, the circumference of which is lined on the outside with branches of trees to give shade to the dancers. Each dancer has a certain place in the dance hall which he must keep throughout the duration of the dance when he enters it. Two small poles or young saplings of pine or cottonwood are placed on each side of the dancer. . . . If the dancer is a medicine man or has been wounded in battle sometime he should show this on the poles or saplings by painting them red, which signified his blood was lost in battle. The center pole which should always be a cottonwood was chosen by the originators of the dance because of its superiority over all other trees as a dry land tree growing with little or no water. This tree represents God. . . .

The sun dance has been handed down to my people for generations as a sacred dance in which we may pray to God, our Father, for those who may be sick, that they may be healed. In many cases, I can truthfully state, many have been cured of long standing illnesses through their faith in prayer and fasting from food and water for the duration of the dance, which generally lasts three or four days. . . .

My people, the indians, worship this same Being as that worshipped by our white brothers, but only in our own way and in our beliefs, which I know is very strange to the white people. But this is the only form of worship the red man, my people, have known for generations past and is known throughout the indian race as the indians' church. Every indian tribe has its own form of worship which is somewhat different, but I wish to explain that they all worship the same Being, God, our Father above. I am told that many years ago some tribes of indians used drastic forms of worship in which they signified their bravery and fearlessness, but these forms of worship have long since vanished. We hear of them only through indian tradition. . . .

I shall state here that the term "our Father" is used in place of God, as there is no

The sun dance, demonstrated here, is performed to heal the sick, promote the regrowth of the land, and for other blessings.

Shoshone word which signifies the word "God." This word is an English word. Therefore, if an indian or interpreter must use this word he repeats the word "God" in English and not indian. Never once have I heard the indian tradition where there was any religious controversy as to the true form of worship of God or our Father. All indians, so far as I have ever heard, believe and worship in this one form.

Quoted in Grace Raymond Hebard, *Washakie*. Cleveland, OH: Arthur H. Clark, 1930.

 ## Red Jacket Defends His Tribe's Beliefs

Efforts by white settlers to force their cultural and religious beliefs on Native Americans have been a source of conflict between the two cultures ever since they

first came into contact with one another. In this powerful 1805 speech, Red Jacket, a Seneca chief, rebuffs a Boston missionary who wants to convert the Seneca to Christianity.

Brother! Our seats were once large, and yours were very small. You have now become a great people, and we have scarcely a place left to spread our blankets. You have got our country, but you are not satisfied. You want to force your religion upon us.

Brother! Continue to listen. You say that you are sent to instruct us how to worship the Great Spirit agreeably to his mind; and if we do not take hold of the religion which you white people teach we shall be unhappy hereafter. You say that you are right, and we are lost. How do you know this to be true? We understand that your religion is written in a book. If it was intended for us as well as for you, why has not the Great Spirit given it to us; and not only to us, but why did he not give to our forefathers the knowledge of that book, with the means of understanding it rightly? We only know what you tell us about it. How shall we know when to believe, being so often deceived by the white people?

Brother! You say there is but one way to worship and serve the Great Spirit. If there is but one religion, why do you white people differ so much about it? Why not all agree, as you can all read the book?

Brother! We do not understand these things. We are told that your religion was given to your forefathers and has been handed down, father to son. We also have a religion which was given to our forefathers, and has been handed down to us, their children. We worship that way. It teaches us to be thankful for all the favors we received, to love each other, and to be united. We never quarrel about religion.

Brother! The Great Spirit has made us all. But he has made a great difference between his white and red children. He has given us a different complexion and different customs. To you he has given the arts; to these he has not opened our eyes. We know these things to be true. Since he has made so great a difference between us in other things, why may not we conclude that he has given us a different religion, according to our understanding? The Great Spirit does right. He knows what is best for his children. We are satisfied.

Brother! We do not wish to destroy your religion, or to take it from you. We only want to enjoy our own. . . .

Brother! You have now heard our answer to your talk, and this is all we have to say at present. As we are going to part, we will come and take you by the hand, and hope the Great Spirit will protect you on your journey, and return you safe to your friends.

Quoted in William L. Stone, *The Life and Times of Sa-Go-Ye-Wat-Ha (Red Jacket)*. New York: Wiley & Putnam, 1841.

"Savage" Traditions?

In his travels through North America in the mid-1800s, artist George Catlin spent time with many Indian tribes. In the following excerpt, Catlin describes the rebuke he received from one Indian after accusing his tribe of using cruel forms of punishment on prisoners. The unnamed Indian replied that white men's idea of justice is far crueler, citing how whites hang criminals and whip their children. At the end of the conversation, Catlin is left wondering whose traditions are most "savage."

On an occasion when I had interrogated a Sioux chief, on the Upper Missouri, about their Government—their punishments and tortures of prisoners, for which I had freely condemned them for the cruelty of the practice, he took occasion when I had got through, to ask *me* some questions relative to modes in the *civilized world,* which, with his comments upon them, were nearly as follow; and struck me, as I think they must every one, with great force.

"Among white people, nobody ever take your wife—take your children—take your mother, cut off nose—cut eyes out—burn to death?" No! "Then *you* no cut off nose—*you* no cut out eyes—*you* no burn to death—very good."

He also told me he had often heard that white people hung their criminals by the neck and choked them to death like dogs, and those their own people; to which I answered, "yes." He then told me

he had learned that they shut each other up in prisons, where they keep them a great part of their lives *because they can't pay money!* I replied in the affirmative to this, which occasioned great surprise and excessive laughter, even amongst the women. He told me that he had been to our Fort, at Council Bluffs, where we had a great many warriors and braves, and he saw three of them taken out on the prairie and tied to a post and whipped almost to death, and he had been told that they submit to all this to get a little money, "yes." He said he had been told, that when all the white people were born, their white *medicine-men* had to stand by and look on—that in the Indian country the women would not allow that—they would be ashamed—that he had been along the Frontier, and a good deal amongst the white people, and he had seen them whip their little children—a thing that is very cruel—he had heard also, from several white *medicine-men,* that the Great Spirit of the white people was the child of a white woman, and that he was at last put to death by the white people! This seemed to be a thing that he had not been able to comprehend, and he concluded by saying, "the Indians' Great Spirit got no mother—the Indians no kill him, he never die." He put me a chapter of other questions, as to the trespass of the white people on their lands—their continual corruption of the morals of their women—and digging open the Indians' graves to get their bones, &c. To all of which I was compelled to reply in the affirmative, and quite glad to close my notebook, and quietly to escape from the throng that had collected around me, and saying (though to myself and silently), that these and an hundred other vices belong to the civilized world, and are practiced upon (but certainly, in no instance, reciprocated by) the "cruel and relentless savage."

George Catlin, *Illustrations of the Manners, Customs, and Conditions of the North American Indians.* London: Henry G. Bohn, 1848.

Chapter 2

Early Encounters Between Native Americans and Whites

Christopher Columbus is generally recognized as the first European to journey to the "New World" of North and South America, but he was not the first outsider to do so. The Cherokee oral tradition tells of encounters with "black" men, possibly Africans, who arrived by sea before Columbus and were driven away. Many scholars believe that Europeans may have visited present-day Newfoundland as early as 1436. And the Vikings are believed to have reached North America in the eleventh century, nearly five hundred years before Columbus.

What sets Columbus apart from these earlier explorers is that his voyage marked a monumental turning point for the indigenous peoples of North America. When the great powers of Europe learned of Columbus's "discovery," they sent conquistadores and colonists to claim parts of the New World for themselves. For Native Americans, the most harmful consequence of these first encounters was that the Europeans brought new diseases, such as smallpox and measles, that Native Americans had no natural defenses

against. These diseases wiped out entire tribes. Historians estimate that the pre-Columbian population of North America was between 10 million and 25 million. By 1900, there were just 250,000 Native Americans living in the United States. Of course, warfare and mistreatment by white settlers also account for much of this decline.

It is an oversimplification to say that Columbus made "first contact" with Native Americans because in reality there were many first encounters between whites and different groups of natives, and they occurred over the course of many decades. For example, Spanish troops under the leadership of Hernán Cortés had conquered the Aztecs in Mexico by 1521, but many tribes along the Atlantic Coast of North America did not encounter Europeans until the first decades of the seventeenth century. Some American Indians of the Great Plains and California did not encounter whites until more than one hundred years after that. When Meriwether Lewis and William Clark made their transcontinental journey between 1804 and

Hernán Cortés and his troops conquered the Aztecs of Mexico by the early sixteenth century.

1806, they encountered several tribes that did not have firsthand knowledge of whites.

Moreover, each first encounter between American Indians and whites was different. Some Native Americans met troops seeking to subjugate them; others met missionaries seeking to convert them to Christianity, or traders seeking to do business with them. Some colonists sought to live side by side with the Indians, and there were many instances of friendship between Indians and whites.

As more and more settlers arrived in North America, however, they occupied more and more land. This led to increased tensions between Indians and whites, which in some cases erupted into war. This process—a period of initial friendship, followed by disputes over land, and finally war—was repeated throughout the colonial period. After the American Revolution, the U.S. government would similarly seek peace with various tribes, only to go to war with them later as the nation expanded. The documents in this chapter explore the early phases of this process by which whites gradually displaced the indigenous peoples of North America.

Columbus

Christopher Columbus wrote a daily account of his journeys to the Americas, but unfortunately this journal was lost. The Spanish priest Bartolomé de Las Casas had access to the diary prior to its disappearance and wrote an abstract of it in which he incorporated many direct quotes from "the Admiral," as Columbus was called.

The passages below detail one of Columbus's first meetings with Native Americans, which the Spanish called Indians because they dubbed portions of the New World the "Indies." The natives he met were actually the Taino. Columbus's notion of European cultural superiority is clearly evident in this account.

Sunday, 16th of December.

Presently more than five hundred natives with their king came to the shore opposite the ships, which were anchored very close to the land. Presently one by one, then many by many, came to the ship without bringing anything with them, except that some had a few grains of very fine gold in their ears and noses, which they readily gave away. The Admiral ordered them all to be well treated; and he says: "for they are the best people in the world, and the gentlest; and above all I entertain the hope in our Lord that your Highnesses will make them all Christians, and that they will be all your subjects, for as yours I hold them." He also saw that they all treated the king with respect, who was on the sea-shore. The Admiral sent him a present, which he received in great state. . . . This king, and all the others, go naked as their mothers bore them, as do the women without any covering, and these were the most beautiful men and women that had yet been met with. They are fairly white, and if they were clothed and protected from the sun and air, they would be almost as fair as people in Spain. . . .

In the afternoon the king came on board the ship, where the Admiral received him in due form, and caused him to be told that the ships belonged to the Sovereigns of Castille [the capital province of Spain], who were the greatest Princes in the world. But neither the Indians who were on board, who acted as interpreters, nor the king, believed a word of it. They maintained that the Spaniards came from heaven, and that the Sovereigns of Castille must be in heaven, and not in this world. They placed Spanish food before the king to eat, and he ate a mouthful, and gave the rest to his councillors and tutor, and to the rest who came with him.

On returning to Spain, Columbus reported this encounter to King Ferdinand and Queen Isabella.

Your Highnesses may believe that these lands are so good and fertile, especially these of the island of Espanola, that there is no one who would know how to describe them, and no one who could believe if he had not seen them. And your Highnesses may believe that this island, and all the others, are as much yours as Castille. Here there is only wanting a settlement and the order to the people to do what is required. For I, with the force I have under me, which is not large, could march over all these islands without opposition. I have seen only three sailors land, without wishing to do harm, and a multitude of Indians fled before them. They have no arms, and are without warlike instincts; they all go naked, and are so timid that a thousand would not stand before three of our men. So that they are good to be ordered about, to work and sow, and do all that may be necessary, and to build towns, and they should be taught to go about clothed and to adopt our customs.

Christopher Columbus, The Journal of Christopher Columbus (during his first voyage, 1492–1493) and Documents Relating to the Voyages of John Cabot and Gaspar Corte Real. New York: Franklin, 1893.

 ## Spanish Address to Native Americans

In keeping with the teaching of the Catholic Church, Spanish policy required that before war could be waged against the natives of the Americas, they must be given a chance to convert to Catholicism. To adhere to this policy, the Spanish conquistadores read the document excerpted below, called the requerimiento *(the Spanish word for requirement), to the Aztecs and the Incas, as well as Native American peoples the Spanish encountered in North America.*

The document states that God created all humankind and made St. Peter the first pope. According to the requerimiento, *a pope who succeeded Peter gave the New World to Spain, so therefore Native Americans were obliged to obey and recognize the authority of both the pope and the Spanish monarchs.*

The document threatens violence if the natives do not recognize Spanish authority.

On behalf of the king . . . and the queen . . . , subjugators of barbarous peoples, we, their servants, notify and make known to you as best we are able, that God, Our Lord, living and eternal, created the heavens and the earth, and a man and a woman, of whom you and we and all other people of the world were, and are, the descendants. . . . Because of the great numbers of people who have come from the union of these two in the five thousand years, which have run their course since the world was created, it became necessary that some should go in one direction and that others should go in another. Thus they became divided into many kingdoms and many provinces, since they could not all remain or sustain themselves in one place.

Of all these people God, Our Lord, chose one, who was called Saint Peter, to be the lord and the one who was to be superior to all the other people of the world, whom all should obey. He was to be the head of the entire human race, wherever men might exist. . . . God gave him the world for his kingdom and jurisdiction. . . . God also permitted him to be and establish himself in any other part of the world to judge and govern all peoples, whether Christian, Moors, Jew, Gentiles, or those of any other sects and beliefs that there might be. He was called the Pope. . . .

One of the past Popes who succeeded Saint Peter . . . , as Lord of the Earth gave these islands and mainlands of the Ocean Sea [the Atlantic Ocean] to the said King and Queen and to their successors . . . , with everything that there is in them, as is set forth

Spaniards destroy idols in Mexico in an effort to convert the Aztecs to Catholicism.

in certain documents which were drawn up regarding this donation in the manner described, which you may see if you so desire.

In consequence, Their Highnesses are Kings and Lords of these islands and mainland by virtue of said donation. Certain other isles and almost all [the native peoples] to whom this summons has been read have accepted Their Highnesses as such Kings and Lords, and have served, and serve, them as their subjects as they should, and must, do, with good will and without offering any resistance. . . . You are constrained and obliged to do the same as they.

Consequently, as we best may, we beseech and demand that you understand fully this

that we have said to you and ponder it, so that you may understand and deliberate upon for a just and fair period and that you accept the Church and Superior Organization of the whole world and recognize the Supreme Pontiff, called the Pope, and that in his name, you acknowledged the King and Queen . . . , as the lords and superior authorities of these islands and mainlands by virtue of the said donation. . . .

If you do not do this, however, or resort maliciously to delay, we warn you that, with the aid of God, we will enter your land against you with force and will make war in every place and by every means we can and are able, and we will then subject you to the yoke and authority of the Church and Their Highnesses. We will take you and your wives and children and make them slaves, and as such we will sell them, and will dispose of you and them as Their Highnesses order. And we will take your property and will do to you all the harm and evil we can, as is done to vassals who will not obey their lord or who do not wish to accept him, or who resist and defy him. We avow that the deaths and harm which you will receive thereby will be your own blame, and not that of Their Highnesses, nor ours, nor of the gentlemen who come with us.

Quoted in Robert S. Chamberlain, *The Conquest and Colonization of Yucatan, 1517–1550*. Washington, DC: Carnegie Institute of Washington, 1923.

 Powhatan's Call for Peace

The story of Pocahontas is one of the most well known in American colonial history. In reality, the story illustrates some of the worst aspects of early encounters between Native Americans and white settlers. In 1609 Pocahontas supposedly interceded with her father, Chief Powhatan, to save the life of John Smith, governor of the Jamestown colony in Virginia, after a series of disputes which culminated in the nearby Algonquian tribes' kidnapping of Smith. This part of the story was used in England to encourage settlement of the New World. The darker end to Pocahontas's story is that in 1613, she was held

Pocahontas throws herself on John Smith to save him from being killed by members of her tribe.

hostage by the English during a war between colonists and her father's people. While in captivity she married Englishman John Rolfe and in 1616 was taken to England; within a few months of her arrival she died of diseases that she had no immunity to.

In the excerpt from a speech Powhatan made during these conflicts, the chief exhorts Smith to peace.

I am now grown old, and must soon die; and the succession must descend, in order, to my brothers, Opitchapan, Opekankanough, and Catataugh, and then to my two sisters, and their two daughters. I wish their experience was equal to mine; and that your love to us might not be less than ours to you. Why should you take by force that from us which you can have by love? Why should you destroy us, who have provided you with food? What can you get by war? We can hide our provisions, and fly into the woods; and then you must consequently famish by wronging your friends. What is the cause of your jealousy? You see us unarmed, and willing to supply your wants, if you will come in a friendly manner, and not with swords and guns, as to invade an enemy. I am not so simple, as not to know it is better to eat good meat, lie well, and sleep quietly with my women and children; to laugh and be merry with the English; and, being their friend, to have copper, hatchets, and whatever else I want, than to fly from all, to lie cold in the woods, feed upon acorns, roots, and such trash, and to be so hunted, that I cannot rest, eat, or sleep. In such circumstances, my men must watch, and if a twig should but break,

all would cry out, "Here comes Capt. Smith"; and so, in this miserable manner, to end my miserable life; and, Capt. Smith, this might be soon your fate too, through your rashness and unadvisedness. I, therefore, exhort you to peaceable councils; and, above all, I insist that the guns and swords, the cause of all our jealousy and uneasiness, be removed and sent away.

Quoted in Samuel F. Drake, *Biography and History of the Indians of North America.* Boston: O.L. Perkins, 1841.

 ## A Harvest Celebration

Sometime between September 21 and November 9, 1621, the colonists at Plymouth invited the Wampanoag, who lived on present-day Martha's Vineyard and the Elizabeth Islands, to a three-day-long feast and exchange of gifts. Although this event was probably nothing more than a traditional English festival to celebrate the harvest, it is known today as the "First Thanksgiving." The following account is one of only two surviving records of the event.

Our corn did prove well, and, God be praised, we had a good increase of Indian corn, and our barley indifferent good, but our pease not worth the gathering, for we feared they were too late sown. They came up very well, and blossomed, but the sun parched them in the blossom.

Our harvest being gotten in, our governor sent four men on fowling [bird hunting], that so we might after a special manner rejoice together after we had gathered the fruit of our labors. They four in one day killed as much fowl as, with a little help beside, served the company almost a week. At which time, among other recreations, we exercised our arms, many of the Indians coming amongst us, and among the rest their greatest king Massasoit [the Wapanoag chief], with some ninety men, whom for three days we entertained and feasted, and they went out and killed five deer, which they brought to the plantation and bestowed upon our governor, and upon the captain, and others. And although it be not always so plentiful as it was at this time with us, yet by the goodness of God, we are so far from want that we often wish you partakers of our plenty.

Edward Winslow, December 11, 1621, in Dwight Heath, ed., *A Journal of the Pilgrims at Plymouth (Mourt's Relation: A Relation or Journal of the English Plantation settled at Plymouth in New England, by certain English adventurers both merchants and others.)* New York: Corinth Books, 1963, p. 82.

The Pequot War

The Pequot War of 1636–1637 was the first major conflict between Native Americans and white settlers in New England. English colonists had begun to move farther inland, encroaching upon Pequot and Narragansett lands, and as a result the Pequot began attacking the new settlements. In response, the English allied with the Narragansett, who were traditional enemies of the Pequot, and massacred the Pequot village at present-day Mystic, Connecticut.

In the document below, Governor William Bradford of the Plymouth Colony describes the colonists' view of the Pequot War.

In the fore [early] part of this year, the Pequots fell openly upon the English at Con-necticut, in the lower parts of the river, and slew sundry [a variety of] of them as they were at work in the fields, both men and women, to the great terrour of the rest, and went away in great pride and triumph, with many high threats. They also assaulted a fort at the river's mouth, though strong and well defended; and though they did not there prevail, yet it struck them [the English] with much fear and astonishment to see their [the Pequots'] bold attempts in the face of danger. Which made them [the English] in all places to stand upon their guard and to prepare for resistance, and earnestly to solicit their friends and confederates in the Bay of Massachusetts [the Narragansetts] to send them speedy aid, for they looked for more forcible assaults. . . .

In the meantime, the Pequots, especially in the winter before, sought to make peace with the Narragansetts, and used very pernicious [harmful] arguments to move them thereunto: as that the English were strangers and began to overspread their country, and would deprive them thereof in time, if they were suffered to grow and increase. And if the Narragansetts did assist the English to subdue them, they did but make way for their own overthrow, for if they were rooted out, the English would soon take occasion to subjugate [conquer] them. And if they [the Narragansetts] would hearken to [follow] them [the Pequots] they should not need to fear the strength of the English, for they would not come to open battle with them but fire their houses, kill their cattle, and lie in ambush for them as they went abroad upon their occasions; and all this they might easily do without any or little danger to themselves. The which course being held, they well saw the English could not long subsist but they would either be starved with hunger or be forced to forsake the country. With many the like things; insomuch that the Narragansetts were once wavering and were half minded to have made peace with them, and joined against the English. But again, when they considered how much wrong they had received from the Pequots, and what an opportunity they now had by the help of the English to right themselves; revenge was so sweet unto them as it prevailed above all the rest, so as they resolved to join with the English against them, and did. . . .

From Connecticut, who were most sensible of the hurt sustained and the present danger, they [the English] set out a party of men, and another party met them from the Bay, at Narragansetts', who were to join with them. The Narragansetts were earnest to be gone before the English were well rested and refreshed, especially some of them which came last. It should seem their desire was to come upon the enemy suddenly and undiscovered. . . . So they went on, and so ordered their march as the Indians brought them to a fort of the enemy's (in which most of their chief men were) before day. They approached the same with great silence and surrounded it both with English and Indians, that they might not break out; and so assaulted them with great courage, shooting amongst them, and entered the fort with all speed. And those that first entered found sharp resistance from the enemy who both shot at and grappled with them; others ran into their houses and

brought out fire and set them on fire, which soon took in their mat; and standing close together, with the wind all was quickly on a flame, and thereby more were burnt to death than was otherwise slain; It burnt their bowstrings and made them unserviceable; those that scaped [escaped] the fire were slain with the sword, some hewed to pieces, others run through with their rapiers, so as they were quickly dispatched and very few escaped. It was conceived they thus destroyed about 400 at this time. It was a fearful sight to see them thus frying in the fire and the streams of blood quenching the same, and horrible was the stink and scent thereof; but the victory seemed a sweet sacrifice, and they gave the praise thereof to God, who had wrought so wonderfully for them, thus to enclose their enemies in their hands and give them so speedy a victory over so proud and insulting an enemy.

William Bradford, *Of Plymouth Plantation*. Fascimile edition of original manuscript, published in 1896.

 ## A Micmac Evaluates the French

In the following document, an early traveler to New France (present-day Quebec and surrounding areas), Chrestien LeClerq, transcribes the reply of an unnamed Micmac who rejects the claim that the French way of living is superior to that of the Indians. He argues, for example, that Micmac wigwams are far more practical than French houses. And why, he asks, if France is so wonderful, have the French left their homeland to come all the way to North America? The Micmac speaker

concludes by suggesting that the European lifestyle may be corrupting some Indians.

I am greatly astonished that the French have so little cleverness, as they seem to exhibit in the matter of which thou has just told me on their behalf, in the effort to persuade us to convert our poles, our barks, and our wigwams into those houses of stone and of wood which are tall and lofty, according to their account, as these trees. Very well! But why now, . . . do men of five to six feet in height need houses which are sixty to eighty? . . .

Hast thou as much ingenuity and cleverness as the Indians, who carry their houses and their wigwams with them so that they may lodge wheresoever they please, independently of any seignior [authority] whatsoever? Thou art not as bold nor as stout as we, because when thou goest on a voyage thou canst not carry upon thy shoulders thy buildings and thy edifices [structures]. Therefore it is necessary that thou preparest as many lodgings as thou makest changes of residence, or else thou lodgest in a hired house which does not belong to thee. As for us, we find ourselves secure from all these inconveniences, and we can always say, more truly than thou, that we are at home everywhere, because we set up our wigwams with ease wheresoever we go, and without asking permission of anybody.

Thou reproachest [criticize] us, very inappropriately, that our country is a little hell in contrast with France, which thou comparest to a terrestrial paradise, inasmuch as it yields thee, so thou sayest, every kind of provision in abundance. Thou sayest of us also that we are the most miserable and most unhappy of all men, living without religion, without manners, without honour, without social order, and, in a word, without any rules, like the beasts in our woods and our forests, lacking bread, wine, and a thousand other comforts which thou hast in superfluity [abundance] in Europe. Well, my brother, if thou dost not yet the real feelings which our Indians have towards thy country and towards all thy nation, it is proper that I inform thee at once. I beg thee now to believe that, all miserable as we seem in thine eyes, we consider ourselves nevertheless much happier than thou in this, that we are very content with the little that we have; and believe also once for all, I pray, that thou deceivest thyself greatly if thou thinkest to persuade us that thy country is better than ours.

For if France, as thou sayest, is a little terrestrial paradise, art thou sensible to leave it? And why abandon wives, children, relatives, and friends? Why risk thy life and thy property every year, and why venture thyself with such risk, in any season whatsoever, to the storms, and tempests of the sea in order to come to a strange and barbarous country which thou considerest the poorest and least fortunate of the world? . . .

It is true, . . . that we have not always had the use of bread and of wine which your France produces; but, in fact, before the arrival of the French in these parts, did not the Gaspesians [ancestors of the Micmac] live much longer than now? And if we have not any longer among us any of those old men of a hundred and thirty to forty years, it is only because we are gradually adopting your manner of living, for experience is making it very plain that those of us live longest who, despising your bread, your wine, and your brandy, are content with their natural food of beaver, of moose, of waterfowl, and fish, in accord with the custom of our ancestors and of all the Gaspesian nation. Learn now, my brother, once for all, because I must open to thee my heart: there is no Indian who does not consider himself infinitely more happy and more powerful than the French.

Chrestien LeClerq, *New Relation of Gaspesia, with the Customs and Religion of the Gaspesian Indians.* Trans. and ed. William F. Ganong. Toronto: Champlain Society, 1910.

The Secretary of War Responds to Violations of the Cherokee Treaty

In an effort to preserve peace between whites and Native Americans, in 1785 the U.S. government negotiated the Treaty of Hopewell with the Cherokee of the American South. The treaty set a boundary for white settlement.

The document below is a 1788 letter from Secretary of War Henry Knox to Congress, responding to a letter from Colonel J. Martin, who had reported on white settlers' attacks on Cherokee settlements in North Carolina. Knox is outraged that white settlers have violated the terms of the Hopewell Treaty, and he states outright that their aggression is based simply on a desire for more land. Knox believes that the United States must honor its treaties if it is to be taken seriously as a nation. Unfortunately for the Native Americans, the U.S. government failed to adopt Knox's fair-minded views on Indian policy.

Secretary of War Henry Knox opposed violations of the Hopewell Treaty and urged Congress to honor its promises to Native Americans.

That it appears by former evidence submitted to Congress as well as by the letter of the 15th of June last from colonel J Martin that the white inhabitants on the frontiers of North Carolina in the vicinity of Chota on the Tenessee river, have frequently committed the most unprovoked and direct outrages against the Cherokee indians.

That this unworthy conduct is an open violation of the treaty of peace made by the

United States with the said indians at Hopewell on the Keowee the 30th of November 1785.

That the said enormities have arisen at length to such an height as to amount to an actual although informal war of the said white inhabitants against the said Cherokees.

That the unjustifiable conduct of the said inhabitants has most probably been dictated by the avaricious [greedy] desire of obtaining the fertile lands possessed by the said indians. . . .

That in order to vindicate the sovereignty [independence] of the Union from reproach [criticism], your secretary is of opinion, that, the sentiments, and decision, of Congress should be fully expressed to the said white inhabitants, who have so flagitiously [shamefully] stained the American name.

That the agent of indian affairs should disperse among the said people a proclamation to be issued by Congress on the subject. That the said proclamation should recite such parts of said treaty as are obligatory on the Union and a declaration of the firm determination of Congress to enforce the same. That all persons who have settled on any of the said lands unless the same shall have been fairly purchased of the said indians shall be warned at their peril to depart previously to a day to be affixed. . . .

Your Secretary begs leave to observe that he is utterly at a loss to devise any other mode of correcting effectually the evils specified than the one herein proposed. That he conceives it of the highest importance to the peace of the frontiers that all the indian tribes should rely with security on the treaties they

have made or shall make with the United States. That unless this shall be the case the powerful tribes of the Creeks Choctaws and Chickesaws will be able to keep the frontiers of the southern states constantly embroiled with hostilities, and that all the other tribes will have good grounds not only according to their own opinions but according to the impartial judgements of the civilized part of the human race for waging perpetual war against the citizens of the United States.

All which is humbly submitted to Congress.

H Knox
War Office July 18, 1788.

Henry Knox, Report of Secretary of War on Letter of Cd. J. Martin, 1788.

 ## Iroquois Relations with the Newly Formed United States

Mohawk chief Joseph Brant, also called Thayendanegea, was a skilled diplomat and orator who dealt first with the British and helped orchestrate the Iroquois Confederacy's alliance with the British during the American Revolution. After the Revolution he worked for peace between the Iroquois and the United States. In this excerpt from a speech he made in 1794, Brant reminds U.S. representatives that the Iroquois desire peace, but he says that peace has been hampered by Americans' failure to honor the treaties their government has made with the Iroquois. He notes that he and other Iroquois have been patiently petitioning Congress on behalf of the Indians, but that their "patience is now entirely worn out."

Brother: At the first treaty, after the conclusion of the war between you and Great Britain . . . your commissioners conducted the business as it to them seemed best; they pointed out a line of division, and then confirmed it; after this, they held out that our country was ceded to them by the King; this confused the chiefs who attended there, and prevented them from making any reply to the contrary; still holding out, if we did not consent to it, their warriors were at their back, and that we would get no further protection from Great Britain. This has ever been held out to us, by the commissioners from Congress; at all the treaties held with us since the peace, at Fort McIntosh, at Rocky River, and every other meeting held, the idea was still the same.

Brother: This has been the case from time to time. Peace has not taken place, because you have held up these ideas. . . .

Brother: We, the Six Nations [of the Iroquois Confederacy], have been exerting ourselves to keep peace since the conclusion of the war; we think it would be best for both parties; we advised the confederate nations to request a meeting, about half way between us and the United States, in order that such steps might be taken as would bring about a peace; this request was made, and Congress appointed commissioners to meet us at Muskingum [Ohio], which we agreed to, a boundary line was then proposed by us, and refused by Governor St. Clair, one of your commissioners. The Wyandots, a few Delawares, and some others [who were not part of the Iroquois Confederacy], met the commissioners, though not authorized, and confirmed the lines of what was not their property, but a common to all nations. . . .

Brother: You must recollect the number of chiefs who have, at divers times, waited on Congress; they have pointed out the means to be taken, and held out the same language, uniformly, at one time as another; that was, if you would withdraw your claim to the boundary line, and lands within the line, as offered by us; had this been done, peace would have taken place; and, unless this still be done, we see no other method of accomplishing it.

Brother: We have borne everything patiently for this long time past; we have done everything we could consistently do with the welfare of our nations in general—notwithstanding the many advantages that have been taken of us, by individuals making purchases from us, the Six Nations, whose fraudulent conduct towards us Congress never has taken notice of, nor in any wise seen us rectified [put right], nor made our minds easy. This is the case to the present day; our patience is now entirely worn out; you see the difficulties we labor under. . . . The boundary line we pointed out, we think is a just one, although the United States claim lands west of that line; the trifle that has been paid by the United States can be no object in comparison to what a peace would be.

Brother: We are of the same opinion with the people of the United States; you consider yourselves as independent people; we, as the original inhabitants of this country, and sovereigns of the soil, look upon ourselves as equally independent, and free as any other nation or nations. This country was given to us by the Great Spirit above; we wish to enjoy it, and have our passage along the lake, within the line we have pointed out.

Brother: The great exertions we have made, for this number of years, to accomplish a peace, and have not been able to obtain it; our patience, as we have already observed, is exhausted, and we are discouraged from persevering any longer. We, therefore, throw ourselves under the protection of the Great Spirit above, who, we hope, will order all things for the best. We have told you our patience is worn out; but not so far, but that we wish for peace, and, whenever we hear that pleasing sound, we shall pay attention to it.

Quoted in American State Papers, vol. 5.

 ## Tecumseh's Call to War

By 1811 Tecumseh, a Shawnee warrior, had become convinced that Native Americans had to unite in order stop the westward advance of European settlers. He embarked on a six-month mission to unite the remaining free tribes east of the Mississippi. In the speech below, Tecumseh appeals to the bravery of the Choctaw and Chickasaw tribes, who are reluctant to go to war with the whites. He warns that if they do not make a stand now, the whites will eventually conquer them and take their lands.

While Tecumseh traveled south to speak to the Choctaw and Chickasaw, William

Henry Harrison, the territorial governor of Ohio, attacked and burned Tecumseh's forces at the Battle of Tippecanoe. Tecumseh's crusade ended almost before it began, but his predictions about white expansion proved accurate.

In view of questions of vast importance, have we met together in solemn council tonight. Nor should we here debate whether we have been wronged and injured, but by what measures we should avenge ourselves; for our merciless oppressors, having long since planned out their proceedings, are not about to make, but have and are still making attacks upon our race who have as yet come to no resolution. . . . The whites are already nearly a match for us all united, and too strong for any one tribe alone to resist; so that unless we support one another with our collective and united forces; unless every tribe unanimously combines to give check to the ambition and avarice [greed] of the whites, they will soon conquer us apart and disunited, and we will be driven away from our native country and scattered as autumnal leaves before the wind.

But have we not courage enough remaining to defend our country and maintain our ancient independence? Will we calmly suffer the white intruders and tyrants to enslave us? Shall it be said of our race that we knew not how to extricate [remove] ourselves from the three most dreadful calamities—folly [foolishness], inactivity and cowardice? But what need is there to speak of the past? It speaks for itself and asks, Where today is the Pequod [Pequot]? Where the Narragansetts, the Mohawks, Pocanokets, and many other once

Tecumseh called for Native Americans to fight against the settlers' expansion into their territory.

powerful tribes of our race? They have vanished before the avarice and oppression of the white men, as snow before a summer sun. In the vain hope of alone defending their ancient possessions, they have fallen in the wars with the white men. Look abroad over their once beautiful country, and what see you now? Naught but the ravages of the pale face destroyers meet our eyes. So it will be with you Choctaws and Chickasaws! Soon your mighty forest trees, under the shade of whose wide spreading branches you have played in infancy, sported in boyhood, and now rest your wearied limbs after the fatigue of the chase, will be cut down to fence in the land which the white intruders dare to call their own. Soon their broad roads will pass over

the grave of your fathers, and the place of their rest will be blotted out forever. The annihilation of our race is at hand unless we unite in one common cause against the common foe. Think not, brave Choctaws and Chickasaws, that you can remain passive and indifferent to the common danger, and thus escape the common fate. Your people, too, will soon be as falling leaves and scattering clouds before their blighting breath. You, too, will be driven away from your native land and ancient domains as leaves are driven before the wintry storms.

Sleep not longer, O Choctaws and Chickasaws, in false security and delusive [delusionary] hopes. Our broad domains are fast escaping from our grasp. Every year our white intruders become more greedy, exacting, oppressive and overbearing. Every year contentions spring up between them and our people and when blood is shed we have to make atonement [amends] whether right or wrong, at the cost of the lives of our greatest chiefs, and the yielding up of large tracts of our lands. Before the pale faces came among us, we enjoyed the happiness of unbounded freedom, and were acquainted with neither riches, wants nor oppression. How is it now? Wants and oppression are our lot; for are we not controlled in everything, and dare we move without asking, by your leave? Are we not being stripped day by day of the little that remains of our ancient liberty? Do they not even kick and strike us as they do their black-faces [slaves]? How long will it be before they will tie us to a post and whip us, and make us work for them in their corn fields as they do them? Shall we wait for that moment or shall we die fighting before submitting to such ignominy [humiliation]?

Have we not for years had before our eyes a sample of their designs, and are they not sufficient harbingers [warnings] of their future determinations? Will we not soon be driven from our respective countries and the graves of our ancestors? Will not the bones of our dead be plowed up, and their graves be turned into fields? Shall we calmly wait until they become so numerous that we will no longer be able to resist oppression? Will we wait to be destroyed in our turn, without making an effort worthy of our race? Shall we give up our homes, our country, bequeathed to us by the Great Spirit, the graves of our dead, and everything that is dear and sacred to us, without a struggle? I know you will cry with me: Never! Never! Then let us by unity of action destroy them all, which we now can do, or drive them back whence they came. War or extermination is now our only choice. Which do you choose? I know your answer. Therefore, I now call on you, brave Choctaws and Chickasaws, to assist in the just cause of liberating our race from the grasp of our faithless invaders and heartless oppressors. The white usurpation [illegal seizure] in our common country must be stopped, or we, its rightful owners, be forever destroyed and wiped out as a race of people.

Quoted in Wallace A. Bryce, *History of Fort Wayne*. Fort Wayne, IN: D.W. Jones and Sons, 1868.

Chapter 3

U.S. Expansion and Indian Removal

Thomas Jefferson, the third president of the United States, was very concerned about "the Indian problem," as it was called at the time. The "problem" was that the United States was expanding into Indian lands, and many Indian tribes were resisting this expansion. Jefferson hoped, as U.S. leaders had before him, that over time Native Americans would become "civilized" and assimilated into white culture. However, he also proposed a secondary solution. If certain tribes wanted to maintain their own lands and "savage" culture, he reasoned, they should move farther west, beyond the Mississippi River, where few whites had settled. In 1803 he wrote that his goal for the nation was that "our settlements will gradually circumscribe [surround] and approach the Indians, and they will in time either incorporate [join] with us as citizens of the United States, or remove beyond the Mississippi." Jefferson even went as far as suggesting a constitutional amendment guaranteeing Native Americans rights to land in the West, but this idea was quickly dropped.

For the next several years, the federal government attempted to convince Indian tribes to voluntarily "remove" to the West, but many tribes wanted to remain in their traditional homelands. By the 1820s, U.S. troops were forcibly removing some tribes. Indian removal became official U.S. policy in 1830 with the passage of the Indian Removal Act. This law gave President Andrew Jackson the power to negotiate with tribes east of the Mississippi and to remove them to the West.

By the mid-1830s most tribes had relocated, but some, notably the Cherokee and the Choctaw, resisted. Jackson, and later President Martin van Buren, sent federal troops to remove these tribes by force. Thousands of Cherokee died on the forced march, known as the Trail of Tears, from their homes in Georgia to the Indian Territory. Thousands from other tribes died after relocating to unfamiliar land where survival was extremely difficult.

Tribes that moved west voluntarily did so based on the U.S. government's assurances

Members of an Indian village move after they were forced by the U.S. government to leave their homeland.

that the Indian Territory would be theirs forever. This territory was originally defined as "all of that part of the United States west of the Mississippi, and not within the States of Missouri and Louisiana, or the Territory of Arkansas." Over the years this area was slowly restricted to present-day Oklahoma. In 1889, even this last vestige of the Indian Territory was opened to white settlers.

Modern historians recognize Indian removal as an unfair policy that caused immeasurable harm to Native Americans, and it was controversial even in the 1830s. The documents in this chapter provide a firsthand perspective on the removal of the eastern Indians.

 President Andrew Jackson Proposes Indian Removal

In his 1829 message to Congress, excerpted below, President Andrew Jackson proposed *that a permanent Indian territory be created west of the Mississippi. Jackson framed his removal policy as being for the benefit of the Indians, and he originally proposed that Indian immigration to the West be voluntary.*

Throughout the 1830s, however, the U.S. Army forced tribes that resisted removal to immigrate to the western plains.

The condition and ulterior [unknown] destiny of the Indian tribes within the limits of some of our States have become objects of much interest and importance. . . .

Our conduct toward these people is deeply interesting to our national character. Their present condition, contrasted with what they once were, makes a most powerful appeal to our sympathies. Our ancestors found them the uncontrolled possessors of these vast regions. By persuasion and force they have been made to retire from river to river and from mountain to mountain, until some of the tribes have become extinct and others have left but remnants to preserve for a while their once terrible [fearsome] names. Surrounded by the whites with their arts of civilization, which by destroying the resources of the savage doom him [the Indian] to weakness and decay, the fate of the Mohegan, the Narragansett, and the Delaware [tribes that became extinct] is fast overtaking the Choctaw, the Cherokee, and the Creek. That this fate surely awaits them if they remain within the limits of the States does not admit of a doubt. Humanity and national honor demand that every effort should be made to avert so great a calamity. It is too late to inquire whether it was just in the United States to include them and their territory within the bounds of new States, whose limits they could control. That step can not be retraced. A State can not be dismembered by Congress or restricted in the exercise of her constitu-

tional power. But the people of those States and of every State, actuated by feelings of justice and a regard for our national honor, submit to you the interesting question whether something can not be done, consistently with the rights of the States, to preserve this much-injured race.

As a means of effecting this end I suggest for your consideration the propriety of setting apart an ample district west of the Mississippi, and without the limits of any State or Territory now formed, to be guaranteed to

President Andrew Jackson created an Indian removal policy that he felt would benefit the Native Americans.

the Indian tribes as long as they shall occupy it, each tribe having a distinct control over the portion designated for its use. There they may be secured in the enjoyment of governments of their own choice, subject to no other control from the United States than such as may be necessary to preserve peace on the frontier and between the several tribes. There the benevolent may endeavor to teach them the arts of civilization, and, by promoting union and harmony among them, to raise up an interesting commonwealth, destined to perpetuate the race and to attest the humanity and justice of this Government.

This emigration should be voluntary, for it would be as cruel as unjust to compel the aborigines [natives] to abandon the graves of their fathers and seek a home in a distant land. But they should be distinctly informed that if they remain within the limits of the States they must be subject to their laws. In return for their obedience as individuals they will without doubt be protected in the enjoyment of those possessions which they have improved by their industry. But it seems to me visionary to suppose that in this state of things claims can be allowed on tracts of country on which they have neither dwelt nor made improvements, merely because they have seen them from the mountain or passed them in the chase. Submitting to the laws of the States, and receiving, like other citizens, protection in their persons and property, they will ere [before] long become merged in the mass of our population.

Andrew Jackson, First Annual Message to Congress, December 8, 1829.

 # A Cherokee Speaks Out Against Indian Removal

In this 1830 speech, Speckled Snake, a Cherokee, replies to the news that President Andrew Jackson wants his people to relocate west of the Mississippi. He speaks of the help the first European colonists received from Indians upon their arrival in North America, and of how the colonists soon overwhelmed their former hosts. Speckled Snake expresses doubt as to whether the Cherokee will indeed be allowed to live permanently in the land west of the Mississippi; he says, very sarcastically, that the white man's tongue "is not forked."

Brothers! We have heard the talk of our great father [President Jackson]; it is very kind. He says he loves his red children. Brothers! When the white man first came to these shores, the Muscogees gave him land, and kindled him a fire to make him comfortable; and when the pale faces of the south made war on him [Great Britain, in the War of 1812], their young men drew the tomahawk, and protected his head from the scalping knife. But when the white man had warmed himself before the Indian's fire, and filled himself with the Indian's hominy [a type of corn], he became very large; he stopped not for the mountain tops, and his feet covered the plains and the valleys. His hands grasped the eastern and the western sea. Then he became our great father [protector]. He [the white man] loved his red children; but said, "You must move a little farther, lest I should, by accident, tread on you." With one foot he pushed the red man over the Oconee [river in

Georgia], and with the other he trampled down the graves of his fathers. But our great father still loved his red children, and he soon made them another talk. He said much; but it all meant nothing, but "move a little farther; you are too near me." I have heard a great many talks from our great father, and they all begun and ended the same. Brothers! When he made us a talk on a former occasion, he said, "Get a little farther; go beyond the Oconee and the Oakmulgee [rivers]; there is a pleasant country." He also said, "It shall be yours forever." Now he says, "The land you live on is not yours; go beyond the Mississippi; there is game; there you may remain while the grass grows or the water runs." Brothers! Will not our great father come there also? He loves his red children, and his tongue is not forked.

Speckled Snake, speech concerning Indian removal, 1830.

 ## Senator Frelinghuysen Opposes Indian Removal

President Andrew Jackson's removal policy was very controversial in its time. Among those who opposed the policy were Congressman Henry Clay, frontiersman and politician Davy Crockett, and orator and statesman Daniel Webster. Senator Theodore J. Frelinghuysen of New Jersey gave one of the most impassioned speeches against Indian removal, arguing before the Senate for six hours against the Indian Removal Act. In the excerpts of his speech reprinted here, Frelinghuysen states that Native American tribes have an unquestionable right to their lands by virtue of having settled them first.

He also points to past agreements that the United States has made, in which American leaders recognized Native Americans' land rights.

God, in his providence, planted these tribes on this Western continent, so far as we know, before Great Britain herself had a political existence. I believe, sir, it is not now seriously denied that the Indians are men, endowed with kindred [similar] faculties and powers with ourselves; that they have a place in human sympathy, and are justly entitled to a share in the common bounties of a benignant Providence [gracious God]. And, with this conceded, I ask in what code of the law of nations, or by what process of abstract deduction [reasoning], their rights have been extinguished?

Where is the decree or ordinance that has stripped these early and first lords of the soil? Sir, no record of such measure can be found. And I might triumphantly rest the hopes of these feeble fragments of once great nations upon this impregnable [secure] foundation. However mere human policy, or the law of power, or the tyrant's pleas of expediency [convenience], may have found it convenient at any or in all times to recede from the unchangeable principles of eternal justice, no argument can shake the political maxim, that, where the Indian always has been, he enjoys an absolute right still to be, in the free exercise of his own modes of thought, government and conduct. . . .

Every administration of this Government, from President Washington's, have, with like solemnities [ceremonies] and stipulations [conditions], held treaties with the Cherokees; treaties, too, by almost all of which we obtained further acquisitions of their territory. Yes, sir, whenever we approached them in the language of friendship and kindness, we touched the chord that won their confidence; and now, when they have nothing left with which to satisfy our cravings, we propose to annul every treaty—to gainsay our word—and, by violence and perfidy [treachery], drive the Indian from his home.

I trust, sir, that this brief exposition of our policy, in relation to Indian affairs, establishes, beyond all controversy, the obligation of the United States to protect these tribes in the exercise and enjoyment of their civil and political rights.

Register of Debates in Congress, 6:311–16.

 ## Indian Removal Act

The Indian Removal Act was passed by the U.S. Senate on April 23, 1830. It gave the president the power to exchange lands beyond the Mississippi River for Indian homelands and appropriated $500,000 to carry out the forced-emigration process.

The act was couched in humanitarian language: tribes or nations could "choose" to "exchange" land, and once west of the Mississippi, Indians would be "protected" and "forever secure" on their lands. Within the decade, and only after a great deal of resistance, the Indians had been forcibly removed, at the cost of thousands of Indian lives and at incalculable cost to them in forfeited property.

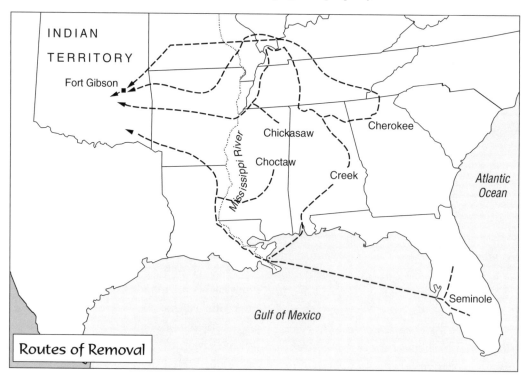

Routes of Removal

Be it enacted by the Senate and House of Representatives of the United States of America, in Congress assembled, That it shall and may be lawful for the President of the United States to cause so much of any territory belonging to the United States, west of the river Mississippi, not included in any state or organized territory . . . to be divided into a suitable number of districts, for the reception of such tribes or nations of Indians as may choose to exchange the lands where they now reside, and remove there. . . .

Sec. 3. And be it further enacted, That in the making of any such exchange or exchanges, it shall and may be lawful for the President solemnly to assure the tribe or nation with which the exchange is made, that the United States will forever secure and guaranty to them, and their heirs or successors, the country so exchanged with them. . . .

Sec. 6. And be it further enacted, That it shall and may be lawful for the President to cause such tribe or nation to be protected, at their new residence, against all interruption or disturbance from any other tribe or nation of Indians, or from any other person or persons whatever.

U.S. Statutes at Large, 4:411–12.

 ## Black Hawk Resists Removal

Black Hawk was a warrior of the Sauk tribe of the Illinois country. In 1804, some members of his and the Fox tribe, with whom the Sauk had become associated, had signed a treaty with the United States ceding all of

Black Hawk chose not to recognize a treaty that ceded his tribe's homeland to the U.S. government.

their land east of the Mississippi. Black Hawk led a group of Indians who did not recognize the cession in resisting encroachments on their traditional lands. In 1832, the U.S. Army was charged with bringing his band into compliance. The "Black Hawk War" ended in July 1832, when the army cornered and killed most of his group. Black Hawk was captured, and while in prison dictated his

*autobiography, of which a portion is repro-
duced here. In it, Black Hawk stresses the
treachery of the white man as justification for
his resistance to removal.*

The white people brought whisky into our
village, made our people drunk, and cheated
them out of their horses, guns, and traps!
This fraudulent system was carried to such
an extent that I apprehended serious difficulties might take place, unless a stop was
put to it. Consequently, I visited all the
whites and begged them not to sell whisky
to my people. One of them continued the
practice openly. I took a party of my young
men, went to his house, and took out his
barrel and broke in the head and poured out
the whisky. I did this for fear some of the
whites might be killed by my people when
drunk.

Our people were treated badly by the
whites on many occasions. At one time, a
white man beat one of our women cruelly,
for pulling a few suckers of corn out of his
field, to suck, when hungry. At another time,
one of our young men was beat with clubs
by two white men for opening a fence which
crossed our road, to take his horse through.
His shoulder blade was broken, and his body
badly bruised, from which he soon after
died! . . .

We acquainted our agent daily with our situation, and through him, the great chief at St.
Louis—and hoped that something would be
done for us. The whites were complaining at
the same time that we were intruding upon
their rights! They made themselves out the injured party, and we the intruders! And called

loudly to the great war chief to protect their
property.

How smooth must be the language of the
whites, when they can make right look like
wrong, and wrong like right. . . .

That fall I paid a visit to the agent, before
we started to our hunting grounds, to hear if
he had any good news for me. He had news!
He said that the land on which our village
stood was now ordered to be sold to individuals; and that, when sold, our right to remain,
by treaty, would be at an end, and that if we
returned next spring, we would be forced to
remove!

Black Hawk, *Life of Black Hawk*. Boston: Russell, Odiorne &
Metcalf, 1834.

 ## The Tragedy of Forced Removal

*Although some Indians complied with the
government's removal policy, others were
forced to relocate to the West. U.S. troops
forcibly marched thousands of men,
women, and children hundreds of miles
across the Mississippi to Indian Territory.
The following record was kept by J.T.
Sprague, an army lieutenant who was in
charge of one such forced march in the
1830s. His account reveals the hardships
and confusion involved in transporting so
many people and the inhumane treatment
the Indians often received.*

The 3rd of September I placed all the Indians under my charge in care of Mr. Felix G.
Gibson and Charles Abercrombie, members
of the Alabama Emigrating Company, and

on the morning of the 5th the Party started for Arkansas, arranged to waggons according to the contract. The train consisted of forty-five waggons of every description, five hundred ponies and two thousand Indians. The moving of so large a body necessarily required some days to effect an arrangement to meet the comfort and convenience of all. The marches for the first four or five days were long and tedious and attended with many embarrasing circumstances. Men, who had ever had claims upon these distressed beings, now preyed upon them without mercy. Fraudulent demands were presented and unless some friend was near, they were robbed of their horses and even clothing. Violence was often resorted to to keep off these depredators to such an extent, that unless forced marches had been made to get out of this and the adjoining counties, the Indians would have been wrought to such a state of desperation that no persuasion would have deterred them from wreaking their vengeance upon the innocent as well as the guilty.

As soon as time and circumstances would permit, proper arrangements were made to secure to the Indians, regularly, their rations and transportation. A large herd of cattle were driven ahead of the train which supplied the Party with fresh beef. Two days rations were issued every other day, while corn was issued every day. The Party moved on without any serious inconvenience, other than the bad state of the roads and frequent drunken broils, until the 22nd, when from the warmth of the weather and the wearied condition of the Indians, I

deemed it expedient to halt for a days rest. Tuck-e-batch-e-hadjo, the principal chief, had been desirous of stopping sooner, and had expressed his determination to do so. The situation of the camp at the time was not a desirable one for a halt, nor was I inclined to indulge him. I ordered the train to proceed. He with reluctance, came on.

From the first days march, I saw a disposition in the Indians, among both old and young, to remain behind. From their natural indolence and from their utter disregard for the future, they would straggle in the rear, dependent upon what they could beg, steal or find for support. I used every entreaty to induce them to keep up but finding this of no avail I threatened them with soldiers and confinement in irons. This had a salutary effect, and was the means of bringing most of them into camp in good season. On the night of the 24th inst. the party encamped at Town Creek, Al., after twenty days march averaging about twelve miles a day. I waited on the contractors and requested them to halt the Party the following day. To this they expressed their unqualified disapprobation and denied my authority to exercise such a power. Their expenses they said were from six to seven hundred dollars per day, and if such authority was given or implied in the Contract, their hopes of making anything were gone. I assured them, that from the condition of the Indians, the common calls of humanity required it, and that one of the stipulations of the Contract was that they should treat the Indians with humanity and forbearance. I ordered the Indians to halt, and told the Contractors they could act on their own pleasure; either go on with their empty waggons—or remain. The party halted and resumed the journey on the following morning, the 25th. The Indians and horses were evidently much relieved by the days rest.

From this period to the fifth of October our marches were long, owing to the great scarcity of water; no one time, however, exceeding twenty miles. The Indians in large numbers straggled behind, and many could not get to Camp till after dark. These marches would not have been so burdensome had proper attention been paid to the starting of the Party in the morning. It was necessary that their baggage, as well as their children, should be put in the waggons, and the sick and feeble sought out in the different parts of the Camp. But this was totally disregarded. I reminded the Contractors that the Party now required the utmost attention, that unless they were strictly seen to, we should not at night have more than half the Indians in Camp. To this they were indifferent, saying, that "they must keep up or be left." Early in the morning the waggons moved off, the Agents at the head, leaving those behind to take care of themselves. Its an absurdity to say, that the Indians must take care of themselves; they are men it is true, but it is well known that they are totally incapable of it, and its proverbial that they will never aid each other. . . .

On the 5th of October I again halted the party and rested one day. To this the Contractors objected and seemed determined to drive the Indians into their measures. The 7th the party again moved and on the 9th

inst. encamped near Memphis, Tenn. Great inconvenience was experienced upon this entire route for the want of Depots of provisions. There was no time when the proper rations were not issued, but from the frequent necessity of gathering and hauling corn, the Indians were often obliged to take their rations after dark. This caused great confusion and many were deprived of their just share. . . .

The Mississippi Swamp at this season was impassable for waggons and it was agreed that the horses should go through while the women and children with their baggage took steam boats to Rock Roe. This place was attained by descending the Mississippi, about one hundred miles to the mouth of White River, and ascending this river about seventy miles, and thereby avoiding a swamp about fifty miles in breadth.

Finding that the embarkation of the parties that proceeded mine would cause much delay, a mutual agreement was effected between the Chiefs, the Contractors and myself, to take the Party up the Arkansas river to Little Rock. The advantages to be gained by this were evident; it put us ahead of all the other parties, secured us an abundant supply of provisions, and avoided a tedious journey of one hundred and fifty miles on foot. A commodious steam boat was procured and upon this and two flat boats I put as near as could be estimated fifteen hundred women and children and some men, with their baggage. The men amounting to some six or seven hundred passed through the swamp with their horses, in charge of my Assistant Agent Mr. Freeman. I received every assurance that upon this route the necessary provision was made for them. On board the boats, an abundance of corn and bacon were stored for the party to subsist upon until we should reach Little Rock. On the 27th the boat started. The Indians were comfortably accommodated, sheltered from the severity of the weather and from the many sufferings attending a journey on foot. The boats stopped at night for them to cook and sleep, and in the morning, resumed the journey.

The current of the Arkansas being so strong at this time, it was found expedient to leave a part of the Indians until the boat could go up and return. These were left in the care of an Agent with the necessary supplies. On the 3rd of November we arrived at Little Rock. The larger portion of the party which passed through the Swamp, joined us the 4th. Many remained behind and sent word, that "when they had got bear skins enough to cover them they would come on." Here, they felt independent, game was abundant and they were almost out of the reach of the white-men. At first, it was my determination to remain at Little Rock until the whole party should assemble. But from the scarcity of provisions and the sale of liquor, I determined to proceed up the country about fifty miles and there await the arrival of all the Indians. Tuck-e-batch-e-hadjo refused to go. "He wanted nothing from the white-men and should rest." Every resting place with him was where he could procure a sufficiency of liquor. The petulant and vindictive feeling which this Chief so often evinced, detracted very much from the authority he once exercised over his people. But few were inclined to remain with him.

The 12th we encamped at Potts, the place designated for the concentration of the whole party. My Assistant Agent, together with three Agents of the Company, returned immediately to bring up and subsist all in the rear. Some of them went as far back as the Mississippi Swamp. They collected, subsisted and transported all they could get to start by every argument and entreaty. . . . A body of Indians under a secondary Chief, Narticher-tus-ten-nugge expressed their determination to remain in the swamp in spite of every remonstrance. They evinced the most hostile feelings and cautioned the white-men to keep away from them. The 14th the steam boat that had returned from Little Rock to bring up those left on the Arkansas, arrived at our encampment with Tuck-e-batch-e-hadjo and his few adherents on board. On this boat the following day, I put all the sick, feeble and aged, placed them in charge of Doctor Hill, the surgeon of the party, with instructions to proceed to Fort Gibson, and then be governed by the proper officer at that place. This party arrived at their place of destination on the 22nd instant and were received by the officer of the proper department. The Agents bringing up the rear, arrived at camp on the 17th. Those in the Swamp still persisted in their determination to remain. Neither the Agents or myself had any means by which we could force them into proper measures, most conducive to their comfort and progress. The season being far advanced and the weather daily becoming more severe, I ordered the party to proceed the following morning.

The sufferings of the Indians at this period were intense. With nothing more than a cotton garment thrown over them, their feet bare, they were compelled to encounter cold, sleeting storms and to travel over hard frozen ground. Frequent appeals were made to me to clothe their nakedness and to protect their lacerated feet. To these I could do no more than what came within the provisions of the Contract. I ordered the party to halt on the 22nd and proceeded again on the 23rd. The weather was still severe, but delay only made our condition worse. The steam boat, on its return from Fort Gibson, fortunately found us encamped near the river Spadra. On board of her I succeeded in getting nearly the whole party, amounting now to some sixteen hundred souls.

Quoted in Grant Foreman, *Indian Removal*. Norman: University of Oklahoma Press, 1932.

 ## Choctaw Removal

The Treaty of Dancing Rabbit Creek, signed by the Choctaw and the U.S. government on September 27, 1830, was the first removal agreement to be concluded after passage of the Indian Removal Act of 1830. Choctaw removal happened in sporadic stages throughout the 1830s. This document, a newspaper account from the 1840s, records the last Choctaw emigration. The article exhibits a romantic, stereotyped view of Indians and expresses a kind of sentimental regret at their passing. The unknown author does not acknowledge that thousands of Choctaw died in the process of moving west, or that the removal process was incomplete—some five thousand Choctaw remained in Mississippi in defiance of the removal policy.

The last remnants of this once powerful race are now crossing our ferry on their way to their new home in the far West. To one who, like the writer, has been familiar to their bronze, inexpressive faces from infancy, it brings associations of peculiar sadness to see them bidding farewell to the old hills which gave birth, and are doubtless equally dear, to him and them alike. The first playmates of our infancy were the young Choctaw boys of the ten woods of Warren County. Their language was once scarcely less familiar to us than our mother English. We know, we think, the character of the Choctaw well. We knew many of their present stalwart braves in those days of early life when Indian and white alike forget to disguise, but, in the unchecked exuberance of youthful feeling, show the real character that policy and habit may afterward so much conceal; and we know that, under the stolid [impassive] and stoic [calm] look he assumes, there is burning in the Indian's nature a heart of fire and feeling and an all observing keenness of apprehension that marks and remembers everything that occurs and every insult he receives. Cunni-at-a-hah! 'They are going away!' With a visible reluctance which nothing has ever overcome but the stern necessity which they feel impelling them, they have looked their last upon the graves of their sires [ancestors]—the scenes of their youth—and have taken up their slow toilsome [laborious] march with their household goods among them to their new home in a strange land. They leave names to many of our rivers, towns and counties and, as long as our State remains, the Choctaws, who once owned most of her soil, will be remembered.

Vicksburg (Miss.) *Sentinel*, February 18, 1845.

 ## The Trail of Tears

The Cherokee called the forced march they endured during removal from their homes in Georgia in 1838–1839 the "trail where they cried." Eventually the eight-hundred-mile trek from Georgia to present-day Oklahoma became known as the Trail of Tears. John G. Burnett was a twenty-eight-year-old private in

the U.S. Army who spoke Cherokee and served as an interpreter during the forced march. The following excerpts are from Burnett's recollections, given on his eightieth birthday, of the Cherokee removal. He describes the many tragedies he witnessed on the Trail of Tears.

The removal of the Cherokee Indians from their life long homes in the year of 1838 found me a young man in the prime of life and a Private soldier in the American Army. Being acquainted with many of the Indians and able to fluently speak their language, I was sent as interpreter into the Smoky Mountain Country in May, 1838, and witnessed the execution of the

The Cherokee embark on their journey on the Trail of Tears after they were forced to leave their native Georgia to go to Oklahoma.

most brutal order in the History of American Warfare. I saw the helpless Cherokees arrested and dragged from their homes, and driven at the bayonet point into the stockades. And in the chill of a drizzling rain on an October morning I saw them loaded like cattle or sheep into six hundred and forty-five wagons and started toward the west.

One can never forget the sadness and solemnity [seriousness] of that morning. [Cherokee] Chief John Ross led in prayer and when the bugle sounded and the wagons started rolling many of the children rose to their feet and waved their little hands goodby to their mountain homes, knowing they were leaving them forever. Many of these helpless people did not have blankets and many of them had been driven from home barefooted.

On the morning of November the 17th [1838] we encountered a terrific sleet and snow storm with freezing temperatures and from that day until we reached the end of the fateful journey on March the 26th 1839, the sufferings of the Cherokees were awful. The trail of the exiles was a trail of death. They had to sleep in the wagons and on the ground without fire. And I have known as many as twenty-two of them to die in one night of pneumonia due to ill treatment, cold, and exposure. Among this number was the beautiful Christian wife of Chief John Ross. This noble hearted woman died a martyr to childhood, giving her only blanket for the protection of a sick child. She rode thinly clad through a blinding sleet and snow storm, developed pneumonia and died in the still hours of a bleak winter night. . . .

I made the long journey to the west with the Cherokees and did all that a Private soldier could do to alleviate their sufferings. When on guard duty at night I have many times walked my beat in my blouse in order that some sick child might have the warmth of my overcoat.

I was on guard duty the night Mrs. Ross died. When relieved at midnight I did not retire, but remained around the wagon out of sympathy for Chief Ross, and at daylight was detailed by Captain [Abraham] McClellan to assist in the burial like the other unfortunates who died on the way. Her uncoffined body was buried in a shallow grave by the roadside far from her native mountain home, and the sorrowing Cavalcade [procession] moved on. . . .

The only trouble that I had with anybody on the entire journey to the west was a brutal teamster by the name of Ben McDonal, who was using his whip on an old feeble Cherokee to hasten him into the wagon. The sight of that old and nearly blind creature quivering under the lashes of a bull whip was too much for me. I attempted to stop McDonal and it ended in a personal encounter. He lashed me across the face, the wire tip on his whip cutting a bad gash in my cheek. The little hatchet that I had carried in my hunting days was in my belt, and McDonal was carried unconscious from the scene.

I was placed under guard but, Ensign Henry Bullock and Private Elkanah Millard had both witnessed the encounter. They gave Captain McClellan the facts and I was never brought to trial. Years later I met 2nd Lieutenant Riley and Ensign Bullock at Bristol at

John Roberson's show, and Bullock jokingly reminded me that there was a case still pending against me before a court martial and wanted to know how much longer I was going to have the trial put off? . . .

The long painful journey to the west ended March 26th, 1839, with four-thousand silent graves reaching from the foot hills of the Smoky Mountains to what is known as Indian territory in the West. And covetousness [greed] on the part of the white race was the cause of all that the Cherokees had to suffer. . . .

At this time 1890 we are too near the removal of the Cherokees for our young people to fully understand the enormity of the crime that was committed against a helpless race, truth is the facts are being concealed from the young people of today. School children of today do not know that we are living on lands that were taken from a helpless race at the bayonet point to satisfy the white man's greed for gold. . . .

Let the Historian of a future day tell the sad story with its sighs its tears and dying groans. Let the great Judge of all the earth weigh our actions and reward us according to our work.

Quoted in Thomas Bryan Underwood, *Cherokee Legends and the Trail of Tears*. Knoxville, TN: McLemore, 1956.

Chapter 4

Broken Treaties and War

The last major phase of the Indian-white military conflict occurred in the three decades following the American Civil War. In the 1840s white settlers had begun crossing the Oregon Trail to the Pacific Northwest, and in 1849 and 1850 the discovery of gold in California and Colorado led to a massive influx of settlers in those regions. To maintain peace in this period the U.S. government negotiated several treaties with the Indians of the Great Plains. In the Fort Laramie Treaty of 1851, for example, the Plains Indians agreed to allow settlers to travel freely through their lands in exchange for annual payments and assurances that the lands would remain in their possession.

These treaties were soon breached. In Colorado, incidents of violence between Indian and whites led the government to confine the Cheyenne of the area to reservations. Cheyenne resistance to this confinement, coupled with racial hatred among white troops, led to the November 29, 1864, Sand Creek Massacre in which U.S. soldiers killed and mutilated 150 Cheyenne, mostly women and children.

The massacre at Sand Creek escalated hostilities in the region for the next several years. The Civil War (1861-1865) was also a factor in these rising hostilities, for two reasons. First, many U.S. military forces on the Plains were sent east, providing a number of tribes with a good opportunity to strike. Second, the economic turmoil caused by the war led the U.S. government to miss many of the payments it had agreed to make to Plains tribes. Often, tribes depended on these payments for survival. Thus in the 1860s Indians attacked ranches, stagecoaches, telegraph lines, and forts. In the much-publicized Fetterman Massacre, Sioux warriors in Wyoming killed and mutilated Captain William J. Fetterman and eighty soldiers under his command.

Violence on the Plains convinced the federal government that all Indians must be confined to reservations. From the 1860s to the 1880s there was almost constant fighting between whites and Indians as the U.S. Army tried to enforce this policy. There were over two hundred pitched battles between Indians and the U.S. Army between 1869 and 1875 alone. The Indians achieved some military successes, such as the famous defeat of General George Armstrong Custer at the Battle of the Little Bighorn in 1864. But eventually the superior numbers and technology of the U.S. military won out. Although there were skirmishes after the Battle of Wounded Knee in 1890, that year is considered to mark the end of the North American Indian Wars.

The Sand Creek massacre, the Battle of the Little Bighorn, and the Battle of Wounded Knee were all major turning points in Native American history. The documents in this chapter include several Indians' firsthand accounts of these momentous events.

 ## The Fort Laramie Treaty of 1851

The Fort Laramie Treaty of 1851 was typical of the treaties that the U.S. government made with Native Americans and broke in the mid- to late nineteenth century. The treaty was signed following hostilities between whites and Great Plains Indians that broke out after the huge overland migration following the discovery of gold in California in 1848. In this treaty, the Plains Indians agreed to let the government build roads and forts through their territory, and the United States agreed to protect Native Americans from "all depredations," or damages, from whites.

ARTICLE 1. The aforesaid nations, parties to this treaty, having assembled for the purpose of establishing and confirming peaceful relations amongst themselves, do hereby covenant and agree to abstain in future from all hostilities whatever against each other, to maintain good faith and friendship in all their mutual intercourse, and to make an effective and lasting peace.

ARTICLE 2. The aforesaid nations do hereby recognize the right of the United States Government to establish roads, military and other posts, within their respective territories.

ARTICLE 3. In consideration of the rights and privileges acknowledged in the preceding article, the United States bind themselves to protect the aforesaid Indian nations against the commission of all depredations by the people of the said United States, after the ratification of this treaty.

Quoted in Charles J. Kappler, ed., *Indian Treaties, 1778–1883.* Washington, DC: U.S. Government Printing Office, 1904.

 ## The Great Sioux Uprising of 1862

During the Civil War, the U.S. government fell behind on supplying provisions and annuity payments that had been promised to the Santee Sioux in Minnesota. Widespread starvation resulted, and desperation, coupled with the traditional mistrust between Native Americans and whites, led to the Great Sioux Uprising of 1862. The Sioux

*killed approximately 700 settlers and 100
soldiers before the U.S. Army restored order. Over 300 Indians were taken prisoner
and sentenced to death. Ultimately, after
President Abraham Lincoln reviewed
records of the proceedings, 38 were
hanged—in the largest mass execution in
U.S. history.*

*The following is Santee Sioux chief Big
Eagle's account of why the uprising occurred. He describes how mounting hostilities first led to a single incident of murder
and then to a massacre.*

Of the causes that led to the outbreak of Au-
gust, 1862, much has been said. Of course it
was wrong, as we all know now. . . . There
was great dissatisfaction among the Indians
over many things the whites did. The whites
would not let them go to war against their
enemies. This was right, but the Indians did
not then know it. Then the whites were always trying to make the Indians give up
their life and live like white men—go to
farming, work hard and do as they did—and
the Indians did not know how to do that,
and did not want to anyway. It seemed too
sudden to make such a change. If the Indians had tried to make the whites live like
them, the whites would have resisted, and it
was the same way with many Indians. The
Indians wanted to live as they did before the
treaty of Traverse des Sioux—go where
they pleased and when they pleased; hunt
game wherever they could find it, sell their
hue to the traders and live as they could. . . .

Then many of the white men often
abused the Indians and treated them un-

kindly. Perhaps they had excuse, but the
Indians did not think so. Many of the
whites always seemed to say by their manner when they saw an Indian, "I am much
better than you," and the Indians did not
like this. . . . Then some of the white men
abused the Indian women in a certain way
and disgraced them, and surely there was
no excuse for that. . . .

It began to be whispered about that now
would be a good time to go to war with
the whites and get back the lands. It was
believed that the men who had enlisted
last [to fight in the Civil War] had all left
the state, and that before help could be
sent the Indians could clean out the country, and that the Winnebagoes, and even
the Chippewas, would assist the Sioux. . . .

You know how the war started—by the
killing of some white people near Acton,
in Meeker county. I will tell you how this
was done, as it was told me by all of the
four young men who did the killing. . . .
They told me they did not go out to kill
white people. They said they went over
into the Big Woods to hunt; that on Sunday, Aug. 17, they came to a settler's
fence, and here they found a hen's nest
with some eggs in it. One of them took the
eggs, when another said: "Don't take
them, for they belong to a white man and
we may get into trouble." The other was
angry, for he was very hungry and wanted
to eat the eggs, and he dashed them to the
ground and replied: "You are a coward.
You are afraid of the white man. You are
afraid to take even an egg from him,
though you are half-starved. Yes, you are a

coward, and I will tell everybody so." The other replied: "I am not a coward. I am not afraid of the white man, and to show you that I am not I will go to the house and shoot him. Are you brave enough to go with me?" The one who had called him a coward said: "Yes, I will go with you, and we will see who is the braver of us two." Their two companions then said: "We will go with you, and we will be brave, too." They all went to the house of the white man [Mr. Robinson Jones], but he got alarmed and went to another house [that of his son-in-law, Howard Baker], where were some other white men and women. The four Indians followed them and killed three men and two women [Jones, Baker, a Mr. Webster, Mrs. Jones and a girl of fourteen]. Then they hitched up a team belonging to another settler and drove to Shakopee's camp [six miles above Redwood agency], which they reached late that night and told what they had done, as I have related.

The tale told by the young men crested the greatest excitement. Everybody was waked up and heard it. Shakopee took the young men to Little Crow's house (two miles above the agency), and he sat up in bed and listened to their story. He said war was now declared. Blood had been shed, the payment would be stopped, and the whites would take a dreadful vengeance because women had been killed. Wabasha, Wacouta, myself and others still talked for peace, but nobody would listen to us, and soon the cry was "Kill the whites and kill all these cut-hairs who will not join us." A council was held and war was declared. Parties formed and dashed away in the darkness to kill settlers. The women began to run bullets and the men to clean their guns. Little Crow gave orders to attack the agency early next morning and to kill all the traders.

Quoted in Wayne Moquin and Charles Van Doren, eds., *Great Documents in American Indian History.* New York: Praeger, 1973.

 ## A Firsthand Account of the Sand Creek Massacre

In 1863, as a symbol of his commitment to peace with the United States, Cheyenne chief Black Kettle met President Abraham Lincoln in the White House. There he received medals and a huge American flag, which, Lincoln and the other officials promised, would always protect the Cheyenne from U.S. soldiers. Against Black Kettle's wishes, many young Cheyenne still engaged in fighting with U.S. soldiers. In one incident a group of five hundred Cheyenne warriors surrounded a small group of soldiers, who were saved at the last minute only by Black Kettle's intervention. Tensions were high, and in 1864 the governor of the Colorado Territory issued a proclamation inviting all citizens to kill any Native Americans not confined within a reservation. In late November of that year, a U.S. Army regiment under the command of Colonel John Chivington killed and scalped approximately 150 Cheyenne and Arapaho Indians at Sand Creek, in southeastern Colorado. Black Kettle was killed five years later in an attack by troops under the command of General George Custer.

This document is a firsthand account of the massacre, rendered by George Bent, a half-Cheyenne who was living at Sand Creek at the time.

When I looked toward the chief's lodge, I saw that Black Kettle had a large American flag up on a long lodgepole as a signal to the troop that the camp was friendly. Part of the warriors were running out toward the pony herds and the rest of the people were rushing about the camp in great fear. All the time Black Kettle kept calling out not to be frightened; that the camp was under protection and there was no danger. Then suddenly the troops opened fire on this mass of men, women, and children, and all began to scatter and run.

The main body of Indians rushed up the bed of the creek, which was dry, level sand with only a few little pools of water here and there. On each side of this wide bed stood banks from two to ten feet high. While the main body of the people fled up this dry bed, a part of the young men were trying to save the herd from the soldiers, and small parties were running in all directions toward the sand hills. One of these parties, made up of perhaps ten middle-aged Cheyenne men, started for the sand hills west of the creek, and I joined them. Before we had gone far, the troops saw us and opened a heavy fire on us, forcing us to run back and take shelter in the bed of the creek. We now started up the stream bed, following the main body of Indians and with a whole company of cavalry close on our heels shooting at us every foot of the way. As we went along we passed many Indians, men, women, and children, some wounded, others dead, lying on the sand and in the pools of water. Presently we came to a place where the main party had stopped, and were now hiding in pits that they had dug in the high bank of the stream. Just as we reached this place, I was struck by a ball [bullet] in the hip and badly wounded, but I managed to get into one of the pits. About these pits nearly all Chivington's men had gathered and more were continually coming up, for they had given up the pursuit of the small bodies of Indians who had fled to the sand hills.

The soldiers concentrated their fire on the people in the pits, and we fought back as well as we could with guns and bows, but we had only a few guns. The troops did not rush in and fight hand to hand, but once or twice after they had killed many of the men in a certain pit, they rushed in and finished up the work, killing the wounded and the women and children that had not been hurt. The fight here was kept up until nearly sundown, when at last the commanding officer called off his men and all started back down the creek toward the camp that they had driven us from. As they went back, the soldiers scalped the dead lying in the bed of the stream and cut up the bodies in a manner that no Indian could equal. Little Bear told me recently that after the fight he saw the soldiers scalping the dead and saw an old woman who had been scalped by the soldiers walk about, but unable to see where to go. Her whole scalp had been taken and the skin of her forehead fell down over her eyes. . . .

Black Kettle and his wife followed the Indians in their flight up the dry bed of the creek. The soldiers pursued them, firing at them constantly, and before the two had gone far, the woman was shot down. Black Kettle supposed she was dead and, the soldiers being close behind him, continued his flight. The troops followed him all the way to the rifle pits, but he reached them unhurt. After the fight he returned down the stream looking for his wife's body. Presently he found her alive and not dangerously wounded. She told him that after she had fallen wounded, the soldiers had ridden up and again shot her several times as she lay there on the sand. Black Kettle put her on his back and carried her up the stream until he met a mounted man, and the two put her on the horse. . . .

Soon after the troops left us, we came out of the pits and began to move slowly up the stream. More than half of us were wounded and all were on foot. When we had gone up the stream a few miles, we began to meet some of our men who had left camp at the beginning of the attack and tried to save the horses. . . . I was so badly wounded that I could hardly walk.

When our party had gone about ten miles above the captured camp, we went into a ravine and stopped there for the night. It was very dark and bitterly cold. Very few of us had warm clothing, for we had been driven out of our beds and had had no time to dress. The wounded suffered greatly. There was no wood to be had, but the unwounded men and women collected grass and made fires. The wounded were placed near the fires and covered with grass to keep them from freezing. All night long the people kept up a constant hallooing to attract the attention of any Indians who might be wandering about in the sand hills. Our people had been scattered all over the country by the troops, and no one knows how many of them may have been frozen to death in the open country that night.

George Bent, eyewitness report of the Sand Creek Massacre, 1864.

 ## The U.S. Army Praises the Slaughter of the Buffalo

In the Indian Wars that erupted throughout the last half of the nineteenth century, one of the worst blows to Native Americans' way of life was the destruction of the buffalo. The railroads that were built across the Great Plains after the Civil War brought white hunters who, in just a few decades, decimated the vast herds that once roamed the Midwest. In the following excerpt, General Philip Sheridan, commander of the U.S. Army in the West, praises the work of the buffalo hunters.

These men have done in the last two years and will do more in the next year, to settle the vexed Indian question, than the entire regular army has done in the last thirty years. They are destroying the Indians' commissary; and it is a well-known fact that an army losing its base of supplies is placed at a great disadvantage. Send them power and lead, if you will; but, for the sake of a lasting peace, let them kill, skin, and sell until the buffalo are exterminated. Then your prairies can be covered with speckled cattle, and the festive cowboy, who follows the hunter as a second forerunner of an advanced civilization.

Quoted in John R. Cook, *The Border and the Buffalo.* Topeka: Crane, 1907.

A group of white men on the Kansas Pacific railway mercilessly kills a herd of buffalo for sport.

 ## The Fate of the Buffalo and the Blackfeet

For many Plains Indians who depended on the buffalo for food, shelter, and clothing, the destruction of the great herds marked the end of their traditional way of life. In the document below, naturalist George Bird Grinnell gives his account of how the slaughter of the buffalo affected the Blackfeet. Grinnell was the naturalist on General George Custer's 1874 expedition into the Black Hills of South Dakota, and he spent considerable time among the Plains Indians. In this account, Grinnell describes how, with the buffalo gone, the Blackfeet are trying to adapt to new ways of life.

These prairies now seem bare of life, but it was not always so. Not very long ago, they were trodden by multitudinous [countless] herds of buffalo and antelope; then, along the wooden river valleys and on the pine-clad slopes of the mountains, elk, deer, and wild sheep fed in great numbers. They are all gone now. The winter's wind still whistles over Montana prairies, but nature's shaggy-headed wild cattle no longer feel its biting blasts. Where once the scorching breath of summer stirred only the short stems of the buffalo-grass, it now billows the fields of the white man's grain. Half-hidden by the scanty herbage, a few bleached skeletons alone remain to tell us of the buffalo; and the broad, deep trails, over which the dark herds passed by thousands, are now grass-grown and fast disappearing under the effacing hand of time. The buffalo have disappeared, and the fate of the buffalo has almost overtaken the Blackfeet.

As known to the whites, the Blackfeet were true prairie Indians, seldom venturing into the mountains, except when they crossed them to war with the Kutenais, the Flatheads, or the Snakes. They subsisted almost wholly on the flesh of the buffalo. They were hardy, untiring, brave, ferocious. Swift to move, whether on foot or horseback, they made long journeys to war, and with telling force struck their enemies. They had conquered and driven out from the territory which they occupied the tribes who once inhabited it, and maintained a desultory and successful warfare against all invaders, fighting with the Crees on the north, the Assinaboines on the east, the Crows on the south, and the Snakes, Kalispels, and Kutenais on the southwest and west. In those days the Blackfeet were rich and powerful. The buffalo fed and clothed them, and they needed nothing beyond what nature supplied. This was their time of success and happiness.

Crowded into a little corner of the great territory which they once dominated, and holding this corner by an uncertain tenure, a few Blackfeet still exist, the pitiful remnant of a once mighty people. Huddled together about their agencies, they are facing the problem before them, striving, helplessly but bravely, to accommodate themselves to the new order of things; trying in the face of adverse surroundings to wrench themselves loose from their accustomed ways of life; to give up inherited habits and form new ones; to break away from all that is natural to them, from all that they have been taught—to re-

verse their whole mode of existence. They are striving to earn their living, as the white man earns his, by toil. The struggle is hard and slow, and in carrying it on they are wasting away and growing fewer in numbers. But though unused to labor, ignorant of agriculture, unacquainted with tools or seeds or soils, knowing nothing of the ways of life in permanent houses or of the laws of health, scantily fed, often utterly discouraged by failure, they are still making a noble fight for existence.

Only within a few years—since the buffalo disappeared—has this change been going on; so recently has it come that the old order and the new meet face to face. In the trees along the river valleys, still quietly resting on their aerial sepulchers [tombs], sleep the forms of the ancient hunter-warrior who conquered and held this broad land; while, not far away, Blackfoot farmers now rudely cultivate their little crops, and gather scanty harvests from narrow fields.

It is the meeting of the past and the present, of savagery and civilization. The issue cannot be doubtful. Old methods must pass away. The Blackfeet will become civilized, but at a terrible cost. To me there is an interest, profound and pathetic, in watching the progress of the struggle.

George Bird Grinnell, *Blackfoot Lodge Tales: The Story of a Prairie People*. 1892.

 A Newspaper Account of the Battle of the Little Bighorn

In June 1876, the U.S. Army was sent to the Montana Territory to remove the Dakota Indians of the area in order to make way

for miners in search of gold. In the notorious Battle of the Little Bighorn, also known as Custer's Last Stand, General George Custer led a failed attack against a large group of Cheyenne and Sioux that were camped in the territory. Custer was quickly surrounded, and in little more than an hour, he and two hundred of his men were dead.

People in the East learned of the battle on July 6, shortly after the country's centennial, in the New York Times *account excerpted below. In the next day's issue, the entire front page was filled with detailed and emotional accounts. The Battle of the Little Bighorn shocked the United States. It was one of the most stunning victories in the Native Americans' long struggle against white encroachment. However, the victory was short-lived; within a few years the Plains tribes had no choice but to surrender.*

Salt Lake, July 5.—The special correspondent of the *Helena (Montana) Herald* writes from Stillwater, Montana, under date of July 2, as follows:

Muggins Taylor, a scout for Gen. Gibbon, arrived here last night direct from Little Horn River, and reports that Gen. Custer found the Indian camp of 2,000 lodges on the Little Horn, and immediately attacked it. He charged the thickest portion of the camp with five companies. Nothing is known of the operation of the detachment except their course as traced by the dead. Major Reno commanded the other seven companies and attacked the lower portion of the camp. The Indians poured a murderous fire from all directions. Gen. Custer, his two brothers, his nephew, and brother-in-law were all killed, and not one of his detachment escaped. Two hundred and seven men were buried in one place. The number killed was estimated at 300, and the wounded at thirty-one.

The Indians surrounded Major Reno's command and held them one day in the hills cut off from water, until Gibbon's command came in sight, when they broke camp in the night and left. The Seventh fought like tigers, and were overcome by mere brute force.

The Indian loss cannot be estimated as they bore off and cached most of their killed. The remnant of the Seventh Cavalry and Gibbon's command are returning to the mouth of the Little Horn, where a steam-boat lies. The Indians got all the arms of the killed soldiers. There were seventeen commissioned officers killed. The whole Custer family died at the head of their column.

The exact loss is not known as both Adjutants and the Sergeant-major were killed. The Indian camp was from three to four miles long, and was twenty miles up the Little Horn from the mouth.

The Indians actually pulled men off their horses, in some instances.

This report is given as Taylor told it as he was over the field after the battle. The above is confirmed by other letters, which say Custer has met with a fearful disaster.

"Massacre of Our Troops," *New York Times,* July 6, 1876.

Two Moons' Account of the Battle of the Little Bighorn

Two Moons was a Cheyenne chief who joined Lakota chief Crazy Horse and his people after being left homeless by an army raid. The following document is his account of the Battle of the Little Bighorn—or the Battle of Greasy Grass, as it is known to Native Americans. This dramatic account illustrates the hectic pace of the battle. It also gives the impression that, for the Native Americans, the battle was a defensive one: They mainly wanted the hostile white troops to go away.

Outside, far up the valley, I heard a battle cry, Hay-ay, hay-ay! I heard shooting, too, this way [clapping his hands very fast]. I couldn't see any Indians. Everybody was getting horses and saddles. After I had caught my horse, a Sioux warrior came again and said, "Many soldiers are coming."

Then he said to the women, "Get out of the way, we are going to have hard fight."

I said, "All right, I am ready."

I got on my horse, and rode out into my camp. I called out to the people all running about: "I am Two Moon, your chief. Don't run away. Stay here and fight. You must stay and fight the white soldiers. I shall stay even if I am to be killed."

I rode swiftly toward [Teton Dakota chief] Sitting Bull's camp. There I saw the white soldiers fighting in a line. Indians covered the flat [ground]. They began to drive the soldiers all mixed up—Sioux, then soldiers,

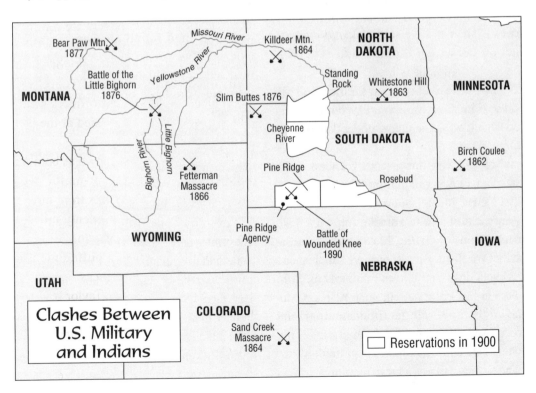

Clashes Between U.S. Military and Indians

then more Sioux, and all shooting. The air was full of smoke and dust. I saw the soldiers fall back and drop into the river-bed like buffalo fleeing. They had no time to look for a crossing. The Sioux chased them up the hill, where they met more soldiers in wagons, and then messengers came saying more soldiers were going to kill the women, and the Sioux turned back. Chief Gall was there fighting, Crazy Horse also.

I then rode toward my camp, and stopped squaws from carrying off lodges. While I was sitting on my horse I saw flags come up over the hill to the east. . . . Then the soldiers rose all at once, all on horses, like this [Two Moons put his fingers behind each other to indicate that Custer appeared marching in columns of fours]. They formed into three bunches [squadrons] with a little ways between. Then a bugle sounded, and they all got off horses, and some soldiers led the horses back over the hill.

Then the Sioux rode up the ridge on all sides, riding very fast. The Cheyennes went up the left way. Then the shooting was quick, quick. Pop—pop—pop very fast. Some of the soldiers were down on their knees, some standing. Officers all in front. The smoke was like a great cloud, and everywhere the Sioux went the dust rose like smoke. We circled all round him—swirling like water round a stone. We shoot, we ride fast, we shoot again. Soldiers drop, and horses fall on them. Soldiers in line drop, but one man rides up and down the line—all the time shouting. He rode a sorrel [light reddish-brown] horse with white face and white fore-legs. I don't know who he was. He was a brave man.

Indians keep swirling round and round, and the soldiers killed only a few. Many soldiers fell. At last all horses killed but five. Once in a while some man would break out and run toward the river, but he would fall. At last about a hundred men and five horsemen stood on the hill all bunched together. All along the bugler kept blowing his commands. He was very brave too. Then a chief was killed. I hear it was Long Hair [Custer], I don't know; and then the five horsemen and the bunch of men, may be so forty, started toward the river. The man on the sorrel horse led them, shouting all the time. He wore a buckskin shirt, and had long black hair and mustache. He fought hard with a big knife. His men were all covered with white dust. I couldn't tell whether they were officers or not. One man all alone ran far down toward the river, then round up over the hill. I thought he was going to escape, but a Sioux fired and hit him in the head. He was the last man. He wore braid on his arms [he was a sergeant].

All the soldiers were now killed, and the bodies were stripped. After that no one could tell which were officers. The bodies were left where they fell. We had no dance that night. We were sorrowful.

Next day four Sioux chiefs and two Cheyennes and I, Two Moon, went upon the battlefield to count the dead. One man carried a little bundle of sticks. When we came to dead men, we took a little stick and gave it to another man, so we counted the dead. There were 388. There were thirty-nine Sioux and seven Cheyennes killed, and about a hundred wounded.

Crazy Horse (left) and his tribe depart for Camp Sheridan to surrender to General Crook.

Some white soldiers were cut with knives, to make sure they were dead; and the war women had mangled some. Most of them were left just where they fell. We came to the man with the big mustache; he lay down the hills towards the river. The Indians did not take his buckskin shirt. The Sioux said, "That is a big chief. That is Long Hair." I don't know. I had never seen him.

Quoted in *McClure's Magazine*, 1898.

 ## Crazy Horse: We Had to Fight

The reputation of Oglala Sioux chief Crazy Horse has achieved legendary pro- *portions as the result of his skill as a tactician and warrior in the North American Indian Wars. He played a key role in many of the most famous clashes between Native Americans and whites—the Fetterman Massacre of 1866, Red Cloud's War of 1866–1868, the defeat of General George Crook at Fort Rosebud, Montana, in 1876, and the defeat of General George Custer nine days later at the Battle of the Little Bighorn.*

Following the Battle of the Little Bighorn, the U.S. Army pursued the Sioux and Cheyenne relentlessly, and in May 1877 Crazy Horse finally surrendered. He was later bayoneted while trying to escape. He gave the following speech before he died. In it, he explains why he spent his life at war with whites.

My friend [the Indian agent Jesse Lee, who transcribed Crazy Horse's words], I do not blame you for this. Had I listened to you this trouble would not have happened to me. I was not hostile to the white men. Sometimes my young men would attack the Indians who were their enemies and took their ponies. They did it in return.

We had buffalo for food, and their hides for clothing and for our teepees. We preferred hunting to a life of idleness on the reservation, where we were driven against our will. At times we did not get enough to eat, and we were not allowed to leave the reservation to hunt.

We preferred our own way of living. We were no expense to the government. All we wanted was peace and to be left alone. Soldiers were sent out in the winter, who destroyed our villages.

Then "Long Hair" [Custer] came in the same way. They say we massacred him, but he would have done the same thing to us had we not defended ourselves and fought to the last. Our first impulse was to escape with our [wives] and [children], but we were so hemmed in that we had to fight.

After that I went up on the Tongue River with a few of my people and lived in peace. But the government would not let me alone. Finally, I came back to the Red Cloud Agency [a reservation]. Yet I was not allowed to remain quiet.

I was tired of fighting. I went to [surrender at] the Spotted Tail Agency [a reservation] and asked that chief [the head of the reservation] and his agent [in the Bureau of Indian Affairs] to let me live there in peace. I came here with the agent [Lee] to talk with the Big White Chief [General George Crook] but was not given a chance. They tried to confine me. I tried to escape, and a soldier ran his bayonet into me.

I have spoken.

Quoted in J. Lee Humfreville, *Twenty Years Among Our Savages.* Hartford, CT: Hartford Publishing, 1897.

 ## Chief Joseph's Plea

The Nez Percé tribe was one of the most powerful in the Pacific Northwest and one of the most friendly to whites. In 1875, however, after gold was discovered in eastern Oregon, President Ulysses S. Grant sent General Oliver O. Howard to confine the Nez Percé of the area to a reservation. In 1877 the Nez Percé, led by Chief Joseph, attempted to flee to Canada and made it more than one thousand miles before Howard's troops captured them. General Nelson A. Miles promised Chief Joseph that his people would be returned to the reservation in Oregon, but instead they were moved to the Indian Territory in present-day Oklahoma.

Chief Joseph spent the rest of his life working to have his people restored to their homeland. In 1885 he traveled to Washington, D.C., where he gave the speech excerpted below. In it, he asks that his people be given justice and be allowed to return to

Oregon or at least to a better reservation. Chief Joseph's plea was denied.

There are some things I want to know which no one seems able to explain. I can not understand how the Government sends a man out to fight us . . . and then breaks his word. Such a government has something wrong about it. I can not understand why so many chiefs are allowed to talk so many different ways, and promise so many different things. I have seen the Great Father Chief [President Theodore Roosevelt], the next Great Chief [the Secretary of the Interior], the [Board of Indian] Commissioner[s] Chief, the Law Chief [General William Orlando Butler], and many other law chiefs [congressmen], and they all say they are my friends, and that I shall have justice, but while their mouths all talk right I do not understand why nothing is done for my people. I have heard talk and talk, but nothing is done. Good words do not last long unless they amount to something. Words do not pay for my dead people. They do not pay for my country, now overrun by white men. They do not protect my father's grave. They do not pay for all my horses and cattle. Good words will not give me back my children. Good words will not make good the promise of your War Chief General Miles. Good words will not give my people good health and stop them from dying. Good words will not get my people a home where they can live in peace and take care of themselves. I am tired of talk that comes to nothing. It makes my heart sick when I remember all the good words and all the broken promises. There has been too much talking

Chief Joseph asked the U.S. government to allow his tribe to return to Oregon or move to a better reservation.

by men who had no right to talk. Too many misrepresentations have been made, too many misunderstandings have come up between the white men about the Indians. If the white man wants to live in peace with the Indian he can live in peace. There need be no trouble. Treat all men alike. Give them the same law. Give them all an even chance to live and grow. All men were made by the same Great Spirit Chief. They are all brothers. The earth is the mother of all people, and all people should have equal rights upon it. You might as well expect the rivers to run backward as that any man who was born a free man should be contented when penned up and denied liberty to go where he pleases. If you tie a horse to a stake, do you expect he will grow fat? If you pen an Indian up on a small spot of earth, and compel him to stay there, he will not be contented, nor will he grow and prosper. I have asked some of the great white chiefs where they get their authority to say to the Indian that he shall stay in one place, while he sees white men going where they please. They can not tell me.

I only ask of the Government to be treated as all other men are treated. If I can not go to my own home [in Oregon], let me have a home in some country where my people will not die so fast. I would like to go to Bitter Root Valley [in Montana]. There my people would be healthy; where they are now [Oklahoma] they are dying. Three have died since I left my camp to come to Washington.

When I think of our condition my heart is heavy. I see men of my race treated as outlaws and driven from country to country, or shot down like animals.

I know that my race must change. We can not hold our own with the white men as we are. We only ask an even chance to live as other men live. We ask to be recognized as

men. We ask that the same law shall work alike on all men. If the Indian breaks the law, punish him by the law. If the white man breaks the law, punish him also.

Let me be a free man—free to travel, free to stop, free to work, free to trade where I choose, free to choose my own teachers, free to follow the religion of my fathers, free to think and talk and act for myself—and I will obey every law, or submit to the penalty.

Whenever the white man treats an Indian as they treat each other, then we will have no more wars. We shall all be alike—brothers of one father and one mother, with one sky above us and one country around us, and one government for all. Then the Great Spirit Chief who rules above will smile upon this land, and send rain to wash out the bloody spots made by brothers' hands from the face of the earth. For this time the Indian race are waiting and praying. I hope that no more groans of wounded men and women will ever go to the ear of the Great Spirit Chief above, and that all people may be one people.

Quoted in *North American Review*, 1879.

Wovoka's Vision of the Ghost Dance

In the late nineteenth century, as Native Americans were steadily losing land to white settlers, spiritual leaders among the Northern Paiute began prophesying the return of the dead, the ousting of the whites, and the restoration of Indian lands. The prophets held that Native Americans should reject white culture and return to their traditional ways. These prophets also in-

structed tribes to perform rituals known as Ghost Dances.

One of these prophets was Wovoka, who in 1889, during a solar eclipse, had a vision of how the Ghost Dance would change the world. He described his vision of the dead ancestors and buffalo herds returning to the earth in the speech below.

When I was in the other world with the Old Man, I saw all the people who have died. But they were not sad. They were happy while engaged in their old-time occupations and dancing, gambling, and playing ball. It was a pleasant land, level, without rocks or mountains, green all the time, and rich with an abundance of game and fish. Everyone was forever young.

After showing me all of heaven, God told me to go back to earth and tell his people you must be good and love one another, have no quarreling, and live in peace with the whites; that you must work, and not lie or steal; and that you must put an end to the practice of war.

If you faithfully obey your instructions from on high, you will at last be reunited with your friends in a renewed world where there would be no more death or sickness or old age. First, though, the earth must die. Indians should not be afraid, however. For it will come alive again, just like the sun died and came alive again. In the hour of tribulation, a tremendous earthquake will shake the ground. Indians must gather on high ground. A mighty flood shall follow. The water and mud will sweep the white race and all Indian skep-

tics away to their deaths. Then the dead Indian ancestors will return, as will the vanished buffalo and other game, and everything on earth will once again be an Indian paradise.

Wovoka, "The Revelation of Wovoka," 1889.

 ## The Massacre at Wounded Knee

In the late 1880s the Teton Sioux of South Dakota embraced the Ghost Dance movement led by Wovoka, who promised the disappearance of the white man. The Ghost Dance movement alarmed whites, who blamed it for several Sioux uprisings. In 1890 the U.S. Army intervened to subdue the movement. On December 14 of that year reservation police killed Chief Sitting Bull as he resisted arrest, and Chief Big Foot and a few hundred Sioux fled the reservation. They surrendered to pursuing troops on December 28, but on December 29, a scuffle broke out that quickly erupted into a massacre. At Wounded Knee, South Dakota, more than two hundred Sioux were killed by U.S. soldiers. The Battle of Wounded Knee (in which approximately thirty soldiers were also killed) effectively ended the Ghost Dance movement and the North American Indian Wars.

The firsthand account of the massacre, below, is by Philip Wells, a mixed-blood Sioux who served as an interpreter for the army.

I was interpreting for General Forsyth [Forsyth was actually a colonel] just before the battle of Wounded Knee, December 29, 1890. The captured Indians had been ordered to give up their arms, but Big Foot replied that

Chief Big Foot lies frozen in the snow after being killed at the Massacre of Wounded Knee.

his people had no arms. Forsyth said to me, "Tell Big Foot he says the Indians have no arms, yet yesterday they were well armed when they surrendered. He is deceiving me. Tell him he need have no fear in giving up his arms, as I wish to treat him kindly." Big Foot replied, "They have no guns, except such as you have found." Forsyth declared, "You are lying to me in return for my kindness."

During this time a medicine man, gaudily dressed and fantastically painted, executed the maneuvers of the ghost dance, raising and throwing dust into the air. He exclaimed "Ha! Ha!" as he did so, meaning he was about to do something terrible, and said, "I have lived long enough," meaning he would fight until he died. Turning to the young warriors who were squatted together, he said "Do not fear, but let your hearts be strong. Many soldiers are about us and have many bullets, but I am assured their bullets cannot penetrate us. [Many in the Ghost Dance movement wore 'Ghost shirts,' which they believed would protect them from gunfire.] The prairie is large, and their bullets will fly over the prairies and will not come toward us. If they do come toward us, they will float away like dust in the air." I turned to Major Whitside and said, "That man is making mischief," and repeated what he had said. Whitside replied, "Go direct to Colonel Forsyth and tell him about it," which I did.

Forsyth and I went to the circle of warriors where he told me to tell the medicine man to sit down and keep quiet, but he paid no attention to the order. Forsyth repeated the order. Big Foot's brother-in-law answered, "He will sit down when he gets around the circle." When the medicine man came to the end of the circle, he squatted down. A cavalry sergeant exclaimed, "There goes an Indian with a gun under his blanket!" Forsyth ordered him to take the gun from the Indian, which he did. Whitside then said to me, "Tell the Indians it is necessary that they be searched one at a time." The young warriors paid no attention to what I told them. I heard someone on my left exclaim, "Look out! Look out!" I saw five or six young warriors cast off their blankets and pull guns out from under them and brandish them in the air. One of the warriors shot into the soldiers, who were ordered to fire into the Indians. I looked in the direction of the medicine man. He or some other medicine man approached to within three or four feet of me with a long cheese knife, ground to a sharp point and raised to stab me He stabbed me during the melee and nearly cut off my nose. I held him off until I could swing my rifle to hit him, which I did. I shot and killed him in self-defense.

Troop "K" was drawn up between the tents of the women and children and the main body of the Indians, who had been summoned to deliver their arms. The Indians began firing into "Troop K" to gain the canyon of Wounded Knee creek. In doing so they exposed their women and children to their own fire. Captain Wallace was killed at this time while standing in front of his troops. A bullet, striking him in the forehead, plowed away the top of his head. I started to pull off my nose, which was hung by the skin, but Lieutenant Guy Preston shouted, "My God Man! Don't do that! That can be saved." He then led me away from the scene of the trouble.

Philip Well, "Ninety-Six Years Among the Indians of the Southwest," *North Dakota History*, vol. 15, no. 2, 1948.

Chapter 5

The Native American Experience Since 1900

Although the Indian-white military conflict was virtually over by 1890, Native Americans' struggle to maintain their cultural identity continues today. The conflict over culture was most evident from the 1870s to the 1930s. In this period, the U.S. government tried to force Indians to abandon their native traditions and religions.

This period of forced assimilation was a response to the Indian Wars of the nineteenth century. In the late 1860s the federal government had adopted a "peace policy" to reduce

Enthusiastic white missionaries (left) discuss their efforts to convert Native Americans to Christianity.

Indian-white conflict. Under the peace policy, reservations were administered by Protestant missionaries instead of the military. It was hoped that these missionaries would convert Indians to Christianity and teach them the basic tenets of white culture, such as private ownership of land, as opposed to the tribal ownership traditional among many Indians. Life on the reservations during this period was often difficult: Reservation police prohibited Indians from practicing their native traditions and forced children to attend white schools.

Gradually, as a result of Indian activism and increasing respect among whites for Native American culture, the policy of forced assimilation was abandoned. In the 1930s the U.S. government turned from cultural issues to economic ones. Poverty is one of the biggest problems facing Native Americans, in part because many Indian reservations are on land deemed undesirable by whites. Several laws, such as the Indian Reorganization Act of 1934, have attempted to deal with this problem, with limited success. In the late 1960s and 1970s the plight of the American Indian received national attention after activists in the American Indian Movement staged a series of radical protests against U.S. mistreatment of Native Americans.

Since the 1970s, the federal government's policy toward Native Americans has been one of self-determination, in which the government works to help tribes manage their own affairs. Gone are the days when the government attempted to outlaw native cultures. But Native Americans today still face a cultural conflict, as they try to succeed in a culture dominated by whites.

 ## The Peace Policy and the Reservation System

The federal Bureau of Indian Affairs (also known as the Office of Indian Affairs, the Department of Indian Affairs, and the Indian Service) was created in 1824 to administer Native American reservations. From the beginning, corruption plagued the bureau, with Indian agents abusing their office and profiting from the unauthorized use of Indian lands by whites. In the 1860s, President Ulysses S. Grant and Commissioner of Indian Affairs Ely Parker proposed a new policy for administering the reservations. They put reservations under the care of Quakers and other Christian churches, in the hope that missionaries would be better able to "civilize" Native Americans.

In his 1869 report excerpted below, Secretary of the Interior Jacob Cox describes the reasons for the new policy and its two main elements: confinement of Native Americans onto reservations and increased efforts to assimilate them into white culture.

The problems presented by our relations to the Indian tribes which still inhabit portions of the western States and Territories are every year making more imperative demands for a fixed general policy that shall give some reasonable probability of an early and satisfactory solution.

President Ulysses S. Grant put Christian churches in charge of reservations.

The completion of one of the great lines of railway to the Pacific coast has totally changed the conditions under which the civilized population of the country come in contact with the wild tribes. Instead of a slowly advancing tide of migration, making its gradual inroads upon the circumference of the great interior wilderness, the very center of the desert has been pierced. Every station upon the railway has become a nucleus for a civilized settlement, and a base from which lines of exploration for both mineral and agricultural wealth are pushed in every direction. Daily trains are carrying thousands of our citizens and untold values of merchandise across the continent, and must be protected from the danger of having hostile tribes on either side of the route. The range of the buffalo is being rapidly restricted, and the chase is becoming an uncertain reliance to the Indian for the sustenance of his family. If he is in want he will rob, as white men do in the like circumstances, and robbery is but the beginning of war, in which savage barbarities and retaliations soon cause a cry of extermination to be raised along the whole frontier.

It has long been the policy of the government to require of the tribes most nearly in contact with white settlements that they should fix their abode upon definite reservations and abandon the wandering life to which they had been accustomed. To encourage them in civilization, large expenditures have been made in furnishing them with the means of agriculture and with clothing adapted to their new mode of life.

A new policy is not so much needed as an enlarged and more enlightened application of the general principles of the old one. We are now in contact with all the aboriginal tribes within our borders, and can no longer assume that we may, even for a time, leave a large part of them out of the operation of our system.

I understand this policy to look to two objects: First, the location of the Indians upon fixed reservations, so that the pioneers and settlers may be freed from the terrors of wandering hostile tribes; and second, an earnest effort at their civilization, so that they may themselves be elevated in the scale of humanity, and our obligation to them as fellow-men be discharged.

House Executive Document no. 1, 41st Con., 2nd sess., serial 1414.

The Religious Crimes Code

As part of the process of Indian assimilation, in 1883, Secretary of the Interior Henry Teller ordered the establishment of a Court of Indian Offenses at each Indian reservation as a means of stamping out "heathenish practices." The rules that were drawn up for these courts were revised in 1892 by Commissioner of Indian Affairs Thomas Morgan, and are excerpted below. The rules outlaw traditional Native American dances and other religious practices, such as the rituals of medicine men.

The following shall be deemed to constitute offenses, and the judges of the Indian court shall severally have jurisdiction to try and punish for the same when committed within their respective districts.

(a) Dances, etc.—Any Indian who shall engage in the sun dance, scalp dance, or war dance, or any other similar feast, so-called, shall be deemed guilty of an offense, and upon conviction thereof shall be punished for the first offense by the withholding of his rations for not exceeding ten days or by imprisonment for not exceeding ten days; and for any subsequent offense under this clause he shall be punished by withholding his rations for not less than ten nor more than thirty days, or by imprisonment for not less than ten nor more than thirty days. . . .

(c) Practices of medicine men.—Any Indian who shall engage in the practices of so-called medicine men, or who shall re-sort to any artifice or device to keep the Indians of the reservation from adopting and following civilized habits and pursuits, or shall adopt any means to prevent the attendance of children at school, or shall use any arts of a conjurer to prevent Indians from abandoning their barbarous rites and customs, shall be deemed to be guilty of an offense, and upon conviction thereof, for the first offense shall be imprisoned for not less than ten nor more than thirty days: Provided, That for any subsequent conviction for such offense the maximum term or imprisonment shall not exceed six months.

House Executive Document no. 1, 52nd Cong., 2nd sess., serial 3088.

Assimilation Divides Native American Communities

The federal government's policy of forced assimilation divided many Native American communities between those who accepted white culture and those who did not. The following memoir by Talayevsa, a Hopi who grew up on a reservation in Oraibi, Arizona, illustrates this tension. Talayevsa writes that, at first, his tribe refused to send their children to the reservation school that was run by whites. Eventually, though, Talayevsa attended the reservation school and was later sent to a boarding school off the reservation. Talayevsa describes his experiences at these schools, and writes that when the reservation police finally forced all the children at Oraibi to attend the white schools, he did not mind.

I grew up believing that Whites are wicked, deceitful people. It seemed that most of them were soldiers, government agents, or missionaries, and that quite a few were Two-Hearts. . . .

Our chief had to show respect to them and pretend to obey their orders, but we knew that he did it halfheartedly and that he put his trust in our Hopi gods. Our ancestors had predicted the coming of these Whites and said that they would cause us much trouble. But it was understood that we had to put up with them until our gods saw fit to recall our Great White Brother from the East to deliver us. . . .

A few years before my birth the United States Government had built a boarding school at the Keams Canyon Agency [a reservation]. At first our chief, Lolulomai, had not wanted to send Oraibi children, but chiefs from other villages came and persuaded him to accept clothes, tools, and other supplies, and to let them go. Most of the people disliked this and refused to cooperate. Troops came to Oraibi several times to take the children by force and carry them off in wagons. The people said that it was a terrible sight to see Negro soldiers come and tear children from their parents. Some boys later escaped from Keams Canyon and returned home on foot, a distance of forty miles.

Some years later a day school was opened at the foot of the mesa in New Oraibi, where there were a trading post, a post office, and a few government buildings. Some parents were permitted to send their children to this school. When my sister started, the teacher cut her hair, burned all her clothes, and gave her a new outfit and a new name, Nellie. . . .

In 1899 it was decided that I should go to school. I was willing to try it but I did not want a policeman to come for me and I did not want my shirt taken from my back and burned. So one morning in September I left it off, wrapped myself in my Navaho blanket, the one my grandfather had given me, and went down the mesa barefoot and bareheaded. . . .

The first thing I learned in school was "nail," a hard word to remember. Every day when we entered the classroom a nail lay on the desk. The teacher would take it up and say, "What is this?" Finally I answered "nail" ahead of the other boys and was called "bright." . . .

I learned little at school the first year, except "bright boy," "smart boy," "yes" and "no," "nail," and "candy." Just before Christmas we heard that a disease, smallpox, was coming west from First Mesa. Within a few weeks news came to us that on Second Mesa the people were dying so fast that the Hopi did not have time to bury them, but just pitched their bodies over the cliff. The government employees and some of the schoolteachers fled from Oraibi, leaving only the principal and missionaries, who said that they would stay. . . .

One day when I was playing with the boys in the plaza in Oraibi, the school principal and the missionary came to vaccinate us. My mother brought me in to the principal who was holding a knife in his hand. Trembling, I took hold of his arm which caused him to laugh. They had a small bottle of soaplike liquid which they opened, and placed a little on my arm. After it had dried, they rubbed

Native American children in Wyoming receive vaccinations.

my arm with a cloth and the missionary took a sharp instrument and stuck it into my skin three times. I proved myself brave enough to take it and set a good example for the rest of the family who were vaccinated in their turn. It was spring when the disease disappeared. We were lucky. The old people said that the vaccinations were all nonsense but probably harmless, and that by our prayers we had persuaded the spirits to banish the disease—that it was Masau'u, who guards the village with his fire-brand, who had protected us. . . .

That autumn some of the people took their children to Keams Canyon to attend the boarding school. . . . My mother and father took three burros and accompanied me to Keams Canyon. . . .

There were a great many of us and we had to stand in line. The agent shook hands with us and patted us on the head, telling us through an interpreter that we had come to be educated. . . .

Then we went to the camp, where my father saddled a burro and told my mother to mount. "Well, son," they [my parents] advised me, "don't ever try to run away from here. You are not a good runner, and you might get lost and starve to death. We would not know where to find you, and the coyotes would eat you." I promised. My father climbed on a burro and they started off. I kept my eyes upon them until finally they disappeared in the direction of Oraibi. I moaned and began to cry, fearing that I should never see them again. A Hopi boy named Nash, whom I did not know, spoke to me and told me to stop crying. My parents would come back again, he reassured me, and they might bring me some good Hopi food. . . .

On June the fourteenth my father came for me and we returned home, riding burros and bringing presents of calico, lamps, shovels, axes, and other tools. It was a joy to get home again, to see all my folks, and to tell about my experiences at school. I had learned many English words and could recite part of the Ten Commandments. I knew how to sleep on a bed, pray to Jesus, comb my hair, eat with a knife and fork, and use a toilet. I had learned that the world is round instead of flat, that it is indecent to go naked in the presence of girls, and to eat the testes of sheep or goats. I had also learned that a person thinks with his head instead of his heart. . . .

By the end of summer I had had enough of hoeing weeds and tending sheep. Helping my father was hard work and I thought it was better to be educated. My grandfather agreed that it was useful to know something of the white man's ways, but said that he feared I might neglect the Hopi rules which were more important. He cautioned me that if I had bad dreams while at school, I should spit four times in order to drive them from my mind and counteract their evil influences.

Before sunrise on the tenth of September the police came to Oraibi and surrounded the village, with the intention of capturing the children of the Hostile families [those who would have nothing to do with whites] and taking them to school by force. They herded us all together at the east edge of the mesa. Although I had planned to go later, they put me with the others. The people were excited, the children and the mothers were crying, and the men wanted to fight. I was not much afraid because I had learned a little about education and knew that the police had not come without orders. . . .

When Mr. Burton saw me in the group, he said, "Well, well, what are you doing here? I thought you were back in school at the Agency." I told him that I was glad to go with him. This seemed to please him, and he let me go to my house to get my things. . . .

The children already at the school were eating their supper when we arrived. Rex and I went to the kitchen and asked for food. We each got a loaf of bread and ate it with some syrup. . . . We ate our food at the door and told the people in the kitchen that the children were coming in wagons. Then we went to the dormitory and rested. The next morning we took a bath, had our hair clipped, put on new clothes, and were schoolboys again.

Quoted in Leo W. Simmons, ed., *Sun Chief: Autobiography of a Hopi Indian*. New Haven, CT: Yale University Press, 1942.

 ## The Trauma of Forced Assimilation

The essay excerpted below is by Freda Mc-Donald, an elder of the Ojibway people, also known as the Chippewa, who today live around the Great Lakes in the United States and Canada. Although there were no Indian

wars in Canada equivalent to those in the American West, the Canadian government similarly pursued an aggressive assimilation policy with regard to its indigenous peoples until well into the 1960s. Here, McDonald shares how this policy affected her. She relates how she was forcibly taken from her family to attend a non-native school, and how because of marriage to a non-native man, the Canadian government does not recognize her as a member of the Ojibway. Since the essay was written Canadian law has changed, but McDonald's experience movingly captures the trauma of forced assimilation.

I hold in my hand a card that I was given by the government of Canada at the time I married a non-Native man. It reads, "Not deemed to be an Indian within the law or any other statute." It is a record of the loss of my identity. It is my alienation, banishment, and displacement from my birthplace and country by the government and its laws. . . .

I was born on an Indian reserve called Fort Alexander in Manitoba, Canada. I was the last of my family to be born at home, coming into the world in the early morning hours of April 26, 1932. My brothers and sisters who followed me were born in the Indian hospital

A white teacher instructs Native American students. This was one part of forced assimilation by the U.S. and Canadian governments.

set up by the government through the Indian Affairs office in the mid-1930s.

Our reserve had long been exposed to the White Man as a result of the fur trade. Following this initial contact, the mukadaykon-ayek, "Black Robes," arrived to convert the Anishnabek "Indians" from their heathen ways. By the time of my birth, the Catholic church was long established, as was the Anglican church. The Protestants settled in Pine Falls, a small town that is legally part of our reserve but occupied by White people. . . .

My parents and our people were self-reliant. They lived off the land. They fished, hunted, and trapped. They also engaged in some small-scale farming and, at the church's urging, grew gardens. The church said farming was a better way of life. Maybe so, from its point of view.

My parents were my first teachers. Parents always are. They taught their children values and traditions in tune with our environment and way of life. We were told to observe animal life, to learn from this, and to follow the rules of the land because this is where we come from. The land is our life and the source of our survival. Everything we own comes from the land. "Look around you," my parents said, "see what we have and know where it comes from." We observed the elements, watched for disturbances to animal and plant life and took these as good signs or warnings because any disruption could threaten our lives. The church called this superstition and paganism. Today, they call it romanticizing and idolization of Mother Earth. To me it was, and still is, simply a way of life. . . .

My generation was the first to receive family allowance—"the beginning of the welfare system." The priest announced that the government had sent application forms to be distributed to all heads of families. Parents were told to list all their children's names and ages and sign the forms. The government would pay five dollars for each child age sixteen or under. This was to benefit all children. Our people did not trust the government or the Indian agent due to past and current broken treaties, so they were reluctant to accept the forms, my father among them. I will not enter into the painful details. What struck my child's mind at the time, however, were my father's words to my mother: "Ageenus, when we take money for what is ours, we give up what is ours for the money. What will happen to our children?" Children hear and remember things. I did not understand the significance of my father's words then, but I fully understand what Dad meant today. It was then that I first felt fear and terror at the unknown. My father did sign under duress. My parents were caught in a stranglehold of coercive bribery.

Mandatory education became law shortly after the family allowances were received. The holocaust of the boarding school and its far-reaching, genocidal attempt at erasing a people began. Family allowances went to the schools. I became a victim, like thousands of other innocent children, who suffered the horror of literally being torn away and cut off from my life source—my parents. I did not know what was happening. They say children are resilient. I suppose this is true, because I managed to survive those long, lonely years—alone and lost! I still ache and struggle, however, to hurdle the soul-searing pain my parents must have suffered at the loss of their children, their family. . . .

I have nothing against either religion or education. These have their place in serving people's needs. I have some fond memories of good teachers, priests, beautiful people I met who gave me help and encouragement to go on. I can read, write, and study words in my dictionary. It was the method used that I find most cruel and morally wrong. We are still living with the aftermath of this holocaust today.

The bottom of my world dropped out when I was handed the card reading, "Not deemed to be an Indian within the law or any other statute" because I had married a non-Native. The stigma of this life sentence entered my soul. This tore the last vestiges of my being into shreds, spiritually and mentally. By law, I could not live or be with my people anymore. I stood alone, once more, but this time naked—stripped of my identity and banished into a world of alienation and discrimination. My roots were severed. I was spiritually wounded. I entered a pit of burning, all-consuming rage! I unknowingly carried this into my marriage. I was sixteen years old. . . .

I walked my road of emptiness, loneliness, and complete isolation. I longed for my parents! I yearned for their love! I missed my brothers and sisters! I wanted my home back. I wanted my community back. I thought of the affection I received from my people. I remembered how beautiful my life had been on my shkonigun. Poor, yes! but full of love— all a person needs to survive. I wept secretly, feeling this great void of nothing. I searched for brown faces on the streets of the towns where I lived in order to assure myself that my people were still around. I longed to run up to them and tell them, "I'm Indian, too!" I was a lost soul, once again a victim of the government's one-sided history and the broken treaties.

When I agreed to set this story on paper, I thought I would sail through it. It would be a breeze, I told myself! How wrong I was! I struggle and weep revisiting my pain. It has become a giant step in my own healing. Truth purges my soul. I hear the words of my grandparents once again, "Waybeenun!" "Throw it away!" My spirit is free.

Quoted in Jace Weaver, ed., *Native American Religious Identity: Unforgotten Gods.* Maryknoll, NY: Orbis Books, 1998.

 ## The Declaration of Indian Purpose

One of the most significant events in twentieth-century Indian history was the American Indian Chicago Conference, a gathering of over four hundred Indians from ninety tribes at the University of Chicago in June 1961. The meeting was primarily in response to the U.S. government's policy, instituted in the early 1950s, of "termination," under which the government no longer recognized Indian tribes as sovereign governments. The conference's "Declaration of Indian Purpose," excerpted below, was the first unified position statement on Native Americans' relationship to the U.S. government. In the portion excerpted below the declaration summarizes the tragic history of Native Americans and calls on the U.S. government to assist the modern Indian community.

In the beginning the people of the New World, called Indians by accident of geography, were possesssed of a continent and a way of life. In the course of many lifetimes, our people had adjusted to every climate and condition from the Arctic to the torrid zones. In their livelihood and family relationships, their ceremonial observances, they reflected the diversity of the physical world they occupied.

The conditions in which Indians live today reflect a world in which every basic aspect of life has been transformed. Even the physical world is no longer the controlling factor in determining where and under what conditions men may live. In region after region, Indian groups found their means of existence either totally destroyed or materially modified. Newly introduced diseases swept away or reduced populations. These changes were followed by major shifts in the internal life of tribe and family.

The time came when the Indian people were no longer the masters of their situation. Their life ways survived subject to the will of a dominant sovereign power. This is said, not in a spirit of complaint; we understand that in the lives of all nations of people, there are times of plenty and times of famine. But we do speak out in a plea for understanding.

When we go before the American people, as we do in this Declaration, and ask for material assistance in developing our resources and developing our opportunities, we pose a moral problem which cannot be left unanswered. For the problem we raise affects the standing which our nation sustains before world opinion.

Our situation cannot be relieved by appropriated funds alone, though it is equally obvious that without capital investment and funded services, solutions will be delayed. Nor will the passage of time lessen the complexities which beset a people moving toward new meaning and purpose.

The answers we seek are not commodities to be purchased, neither are they evolved automatically through the passing of time.

The effort to place social adjustment on a money-time interval scale, which has characterized Indian administration, has resulted in unwanted pressure and frustration.

When Indians speak of the continent they yielded, they are not referring only to the loss of some millions of acres in real estate. They have in mind that the land supported a universe of things they knew, valued, and loved.

With that continent gone, except for the few poor parcels they still retain, the basis of life is precariously held, but they mean to hold the scraps and parcels as earnestly as any small nation or ethnic group was ever determined to hold to identity and survival.

What we ask of America is not charity, not paternalism, even when benevolent. We ask only that the nature of our situation be recognized and made the basis of policy and action.

In short, the Indians ask for assistance, technical and financial, for the time needed, however long that may be, to regain in the America of the space age some measure of the adjustment they enjoyed as the original possessors of their native land.

Quoted in Virginia Irving Armstrong, ed., *I Have Spoken: American History Through the Voices of the Indians.* Athens, OH: Swallow Press, 1991.

Teaching the Indian Heritage

In the late 1960s, a group of concerned citizens, almost all of them Native Americans, established the Ad Hoc Committee on California Indian Education to protest education programs that ignored the Native American culture and point of view. In this excerpt from the committee's 1970 report, the group recommends an increased focus on teaching Native American history, heritage, and culture both inside and outside the classroom.

The Indian heritage should be an integral part of the programs of the school and the Indian community, that the use of the Indian heritage in the school is especially important for helping Indian pupils develop a sense of identity and personal worth (but that it is also important as a part of the common heritage of all pupils), and that local Indian people must be actively involved in any programs developed by a school that touch upon the Indian heritage. More specifically,

1. The Indian people must unify and emphasize their Indian culture, and learn how to retain it and teach it to the younger generation;

2. Indian people should be brought into the school to help professional staff develop materials for the curriculum and to teach arts and crafts, dancing, singing, et cetera;

3. The school and Indian adults and children together should develop projects to record local Indian history, protect historical and cemetery sites, construct exhibits, preserve Indian place-names, and put on pageants; and

4. Non-Indians must recognize that the Indian heritage is a living, evolving legacy which has not been static in the past and is not static today and that the "core" of being Indian is being a member of an Indian community and not a particular style of dress or ornamentation. Teachers must avoid the idea that a "real" Indian needs to dress and act as Indian people did a century ago.

California Indian Education. Modesto, CA: Ad Hoc Committee on California Indian Education, 1968.

 ## The American Indian Movement

In the late 1960s and early 1970s, in what became known as the American Indian Movement, Native Americans engaged in several highly visible protests in an effort to raise public awareness about the past injustices and current issues affecting them. The movement first gained national attention on November 20, 1969, when seventy-eight Native Americans occupied Alcatraz Island in San Francisco Bay, the site of the famous federal prison that had been closed in 1963. The group justified its seizure by citing the Fort Laramie Treaty of 1868, which permitted natives to live on unused federal lands. The island remained under Native American control for over a year and a half. Another confrontational protest followed in 1973, when members of the

A group of Native Americans occupied Alcatraz Island, claiming the Fort Laramie Treaty permitted them to live on unused federal land.

movement occupied the town of Wounded Knee, South Dakota, the site of the notorious 1890 massacre—for seventy-one days before being removed by federal forces.

In the 1970 article excerpted below, Vine Deloria Jr., a prolific Native American writer, expressed sympathy for the American Indian Movement. The title of the article—"This

Country Was a Lot Better Off when the Indians Were Running It"—aptly summarizes the author's views.

On Nov. 9, 1969, a contingent of American Indians, led by Adam Nordwall, a Chippewa from Minnesota, and Richard Oakes, a Mohawk from New York, landed on Alcatraz Island in San Francisco Bay and claimed the 13-acre rock "by right of discovery." The island had been abandoned six and a half years ago, and although there had been various suggestions concerning its disposal nothing had been done to make use of the land. Since there are Federal treaties giving some tribes the right to abandoned Federal property within a tribe's original territory, the Indians of the Bay area felt that they could lay claim to the island. . . .

The new inhabitants have made "the Rock" [Alcatraz] a focal point symbolic of Indian people. Under extreme difficulty they have worked to begin repairing sanitary facilities and buildings. The population has been largely transient, many people have stopped by, looked the situation over for a few days, then gone home, unwilling to put in the tedious work necessary to make the island support a viable community.

The Alcatraz news stories are somewhat shocking to non-Indians. It is difficult for most Americans to comprehend that there still exists a living community of nearly one million Indians in this country. For many people, Indians have become a species of movie actor periodically dispatched to the Happy Hunting Grounds [a clichéd term for "Indian heaven"] by John

Wayne on the "Late, Late Show." Yet there are some 315 Indian tribal groups in 26 states still functioning as quasi-sovereign nations under treaty status; they range from the mammoth Navajo tribe of some 132,000 with 16 million acres of land to tiny Mission Creek of California with 15 people and a tiny parcel of property. There are over half a million Indians in the cities alone, with the largest concentrations in San Francisco, Los Angeles, Minneapolis and Chicago.

The take-over of Alcatraz is to many Indian people a demonstration of pride in being Indian and a dignified, yet humorous protest against current conditions existing on the reservations and in the cities. It is this special pride and dignity, the determination to judge life according to one's own values, and the unconquerable conviction that the tribes will not die that has always characterized Indian people as I have known them. . . .

I wish the [U.S.] Government would give Alcatraz to the Indians now occupying it. They want to create five centers on the island. One center would be for a North American studies program; another would be a spiritual and medical center where Indian religions and medicines would be used and studied. A third center would concentrate on ecological studies based on an Indian view of nature— that man should live with the land and not simply on it. A job-training center and a museum would also be founded on the island. Certain of these programs would obviously require Federal assistance.

Some people may object to this approach, yet [the Federal Department of] Health, Education and Welfare gave out $10-million last year [1969] to non-Indians to study Indians. Not one single dollar went to an Indian scholar or researcher to present the point of view of Indian people. And the studies done by non-Indians added nothing to what was already known about Indians.

Indian people have managed to maintain a viable and cohesive social order in spite of everything the non-Indian society has thrown at them in an effort to break the tribal structure. At the same time, non-Indian society has created a monstrosity of a culture where people starve while the granaries are filled and the sun can never break through the smog.

By making Alcatraz an experimental Indian center operated and planned by Indian people, we would be given a chance to see what we could do toward developing answers to modern social problems. Ancient tribalism can be incorporated with modern technology in an urban setting. Perhaps we would not succeed in the effort, but the Government is spending billions every year and still the situation is rapidly growing worse. It just seems to a lot of Indians that this continent was a lot better off when we were running it.

Vine Deloria Jr., "This Country Was a Lot Better Off when the Indians Were Running It," *New York Times Magazine*, March 8, 1970.

 ## Stereotypes About Native Americans Persist

Many people unfamiliar with Native Americans still hold stereotyped views of them. When most Americans hear the word "Indian," for example, they picture a

nineteenth-century Plains warrior in flowing headdress.

In an essay she wrote in the twelfth grade, excerpted below, Katie Mobeck, an Aleut, writes that when most people think of the indigenous peoples of Alaska, they immediately think of Eskimos. Mobeck corrects many popular misconceptions about the Aleut people. For example, they never lived in igloos, they do not live in a snowy climate, and they do not live on whale meat. Mobeck calls on Americans to go beyond stereotypes and recognize that the Aleut have a distinct, but nevertheless very modern, way of life.

The public has many misconceptions about the Aleutian region's geography and culture. Most informed people could locate the Aleutian chain, but that's about it. Most Americans think that all Native Alaskans are Eskimos: That's wrong. Some think we live on an iceberg. Few know of the Aleuts. The Aleuts are one of the three major Alaska Native groups, but the one that is least known. . . .

The influence of external events on the Aleuts has been great. Even the name of our people has a foreign source. The Aleutian Aleuts called themselves Unangan, meaning, "the people." At the time that the Russians arrived in 1741 there were about sixteen thousand Aleuts. The Russians killed and enslaved the Aleuts; within one hundred years there were only about two thousand.

Nevertheless, we're still here, and things have changed a lot since then, particularly since World War II. We live in standard, well-furnished homes, and we never lived in igloos. At the time of Russian contact, we did live in barabaras: partially underground, sod houses large enough for several families. Since the islands are treeless, driftwood was used for the frame and roof beams. Whale bones were also used to frame.

I am most familiar with the communities around the western tip of the Alaska peninsula. The economy of these communities depends primarily on commercial fishing. They are Sand Point, King Cove, and Nelson Lagoon. There is a substantial Aleut population in each of these three communities. Families in each community are related to families in the other two. Most people of Aleut descent in these communities have Scandinavian or Russian surnames. Scandinavians came to the Aleutians as crew members on fishing vessels, stayed, and later took Aleut wives. . . .

Most think we are knee-deep in snow all year. Actually there is only two to six weeks of snow coverage per year. The Aleutians have a maritime climate characterized by mild winters and cool summers. . . .

Food is another source of misunderstanding; some people think the primary food of all Alaska Native people is whale, walrus, and seal. That's wrong, too. Once sea mammals were essential to the Aleut diet. When sea mammal is available, it is still prepared and eaten in a few communities, but not in those with which I am familiar. Around the tip of the peninsula, commercial fishing has converted us from a subsistence economy to a cash economy; nevertheless, fish and game are important to our diet. We eat a lot of caribou, duck, geese, and salmon. When they are available we have crab and shellfish. We buy pork, fowl, and lots of beef. Although the meat is often not that familiar to an outsider, the menu is usually very American. Today we routinely eat well-known American food such as hamburgers and fries and bacon and eggs, but the hamburger may be half caribou.

So, most Americans need to change their perceptions about the Aleutians and its people. Get your facts straight.

Quoted in Arlene B. Hirschfelder and Beverly R. Singer, eds., *Rising Voices: Writings of Young Native Americans*. New York: Charles Scribner's Sons, 1992.

Index

wars
    Black Hawk War, 49
    Crazy Horse and, 69
    Fetterman Massacre, 58, 69
    Great Uprising of 1862, 59–61
    Little Bighorn, 59
        newspaper account of, 65–66
        Two Moon's account of, 67–69
    Pequot War, 34–35
    Sand Creek Massacre, 58, 61–63
    slaughter of the buffalo and, 63, 64–65
    Wounded Knee, 59, 73–75
Indian Removal Act, 43
    Choctaw removal, 54
    content of, 49
    impact of, 48
    passage of, 48
    Theodore Frelinghuysen's opposition to,
        47–48
Indian Reorganization Act, 77
Indian Service. *See* Bureau of Indian Affairs
Indian Territory, 43–44
Iroquois Confederacy, 38–40

Jackson, Andrew, 43, 44–46
Jamestown colony, 32
Jefferson, Thomas, 43
Jones, Robinson, 61
Joseph (Nez Percé chief), 70–72

Kalispel, 65
Keams Canyon Agency, 80, 81
Knox, Henry, 37–38
Kutenai, 65

Las Casas, Bartolomé de, 29
LeClerq, Chrestien, 35–37
Lee, Jesse, 70
Lewis, Meriwether, 27–28
Life Among the Paiutes (Hopkins), 19
Lincoln, Abraham, 60, 61

Little Bear, 62
Little Bighorn, Battle of the, 59
    newspaper account of, 65–66
    Two Moon's account of, 67–69
Little Crow, 61
Lolulomai, 80

Martin, J., 37
Masau'u, 81
Massasoit, 34
McClellan, Abraham, 56
McDonal, Ben, 56
McDonald, Freda, 82–85
Micmac, 35–37
Miles, Nelson, 70
Millard, Elkanah, 56
missionaries, 77
Mobeck, Katie, 90–91
Morgan, Thomas, 79
Muscogee, 46
Mystic (Connecticut), 33
myths
    cautionary stories, 14–15
    creation stories, 13–14
    of good and evil, 15–16
    in Native American religious traditions, 13
    Raven, 14
    Thunder and Lightning, 15–16
    Trickster, 13–14

Nani, 15
Narragansett, 33–34
Narticher-tus-ten-nugge, 53
New England
    harvest festival, 33–34
    Pequot War, 34–35
Newfoundland, 27
New France, 35
Nez Percé, 70–72
Nordwall, Adam, 88
North America